Memory Training Manual
The Official Field Guide to Memorization from Detective 369

Todd Hearst

Contents

Memory Training Manual

The Official Field Guide to Memorization from Detective 369

Todd Hearst

Version: 2025.08.31 • Built: 2025-08-31

First Edition: 2025

Published by Existential Publishing

Printed in the United States of America

The author has made every effort to ensure that the information in this book was accurate at the time of publication.

Foreword

The fog rolled in thick that November night, swirling around the streetlights like ghosts of forgotten memories. I stood at my office window, watching the city disappear into the mist, when the call came in. Another case. Another mystery. Another chance to prove that no puzzle is unsolvable when you know how to work the clues.

But this case was different. This wasn't about stolen jewelry or missing persons. This was about something far more precious and far more elusive: the ability to remember. To truly, permanently, unforgettably remember.

The client who walked through my door that night was like so many others I'd seen over the years–intelligent, capable, successful by most measures. But there was something haunting in her eyes, a desperation that spoke of too many forgotten names, too many missed opportunities, too many moments when the mind simply... failed.

"Detective," she said, settling into the chair across from my desk, "I need your help. I'm losing pieces of myself every day. Important pieces. And I don't know how to get them back."

That case changed everything. Not just for her, but for me. Because in helping her unlock the secrets of memory mastery, I discovered something that would reshape my entire understanding of what the human mind could accomplish.

Memory isn't just about remembering where you put your keys or what you had for breakfast. It's about identity. It's about competence. It's about the confidence that comes from knowing you can trust your own mind to capture, store, and retrieve the information that matters most.

Over the following months, I developed what would become known as the *Detective 369 Official Standard for Memorization* –a systematic approach to memory training that treats information like evidence in a criminal investigation. Every fact becomes a clue. Every technique becomes a tool. Every practice session becomes a step closer to solving the ultimate mystery: how to build a mind that never forgets.

The methods you'll learn in this book aren't theoretical exercises dreamed up in some academic ivory tower. They're battle-tested techniques, refined through years of real-world application, proven effective in the most demanding circumstances. Whether you're a student facing impossible exam loads, a professional navigating complex information landscapes, or simply someone who wants to stop feeling betrayed by their own memory, these tools will transform how you think about learning itself.

But fair warning: once you see how your mind works–once you understand the elegant systems that lie beneath the chaos of everyday forgetting–you'll never look at information the same way again. Every number will become a potential story. Every list will become a possible journey. Every fact will become a piece of evidence waiting to be filed in the vast, organized library of your enhanced memory.

The investigation begins now. The case files are open. And the first clue is simple: your memory is not broken. It's simply untrained. Our job is to change that.

Chapter 1: The Nature of Memory

Detective 369 adjusts his fedora and flips open a worn leather case file. The streetlights outside his office cast long shadows across the cluttered desk, illuminating photographs, evidence markers, and yellowed newspaper clippings. But tonight's case isn't about stolen jewels or missing persons. Tonight, he's investigating the most elusive suspect of all: human memory itself.

Memory is the detective's most vital tool. It's not just a filing cabinet tucked away in some dusty corner of the mind, nor is it a tape recorder mechanically capturing every sound and sight. No, memory is something far more dynamic and mysterious a living system that breathes, shifts, and evolves with each passing moment. Detective 369 has learned to think of it as a reconstruction engine, a sleuth that never sleeps, constantly piecing together fragments of the past to create the stories we call our experiences.

Whether you're remembering the face of a suspect, the crucial detail that breaks a case wide open, or simply the location of your car keys after a long day's work, memory is what allows you to function in the world. It's your mind's ability to encode, store, and retrieve information–the invisible thread that weaves together the fabric of your consciousness. And while it can seem mysterious, fragile, or unreliable, the truth Detective 369 has discovered through years of investigation is far more empowering: memory is trainable. It can be sharpened. It can be mastered.

This chapter lays the foundation for everything that follows in our investigation. If you understand what memory truly is, how it operates in the shadowy recesses of your mind, and why it sometimes fails you at crucial moments, you'll be prepared to wield the techniques that transform ordinary minds into extraordinary ones. Consider this field manual, your guide through this labyrinth of neurons and synapses, your mentor in the art of mental investigation.

The Detective's Definition: What Is Memory?

Detective 369 leans back in his chair, the leather creaking softly in the quiet of the night. He's spent decades studying the human mind, and he's learned that memory is fundamentally the cognitive system that allows us to retain and retrieve information. It's how we recognize faces in a crowd, remember names at crucial moments, recite facts that solve cases, tackle complex problems, and navigate through both familiar and foreign spaces.

But like any good detective, Detective 369 knows that the surface explanation rarely tells the whole story. Memory operates on multiple levels, each with its own peculiarities and strengths. Psychologists–those colleagues of his who study the mind from their ivory towers–have classified memory into three basic types, each as distinct as the different kinds of evidence in a case file.

The first type is Sensory Memory, which Detective 369 thinks of as the initial impression at a crime scene. It holds fleeting impressions for just milliseconds to two seconds–the brief flash of a face in a window, the echo of footsteps in an alley, the scent of perfume lingering in the air. This is raw, unprocessed information, like photographs taken in the heat of the moment before the brain has time to decide what's important and what's merely background noise.

Then there's Short-Term Memory, or what the experts call Working Memory. Detective 369 visualizes this as his mental notepad–an active holding zone for immediate tasks. It's where he keeps a suspect's description while questioning witnesses, where he holds a phone number just long enough to dial it, where he mentally juggles the various pieces of a puzzle before they either move into long-term storage or fade away like smoke in the wind. Short-term memory can typically hold about seven pieces of information, plus or minus two, though Detective 369 has learned tricks to expand this capacity considerably.

Finally, there's Long-Term Memory–the vast, durable archive that Detective 369 considers his true investigative treasure trove. This is where he stores decades of case files, facts about human behavior, skills honed through years of practice, and experiences that have shaped his understanding of the criminal mind. Unlike the fragile, temporary storage of sensory and short-term memory, long-term memory can hold virtually unlimited information for extended periods, sometimes for an entire lifetime.

Each of these memory types operates on different neural substrates and functions with its own unique characteristics. Detective 369 has learned to recognize their signatures, to understand their strengths and weaknesses, and most importantly, to work with them rather than against them.

The Evidence Files: Types of Long-Term Memory

Detective 369 stands and walks to his filing cabinet, pulling out two thick folders labeled "Explicit" and "Implicit." These represent the two major categories of long-term memory that every detective of the mind must understand.

Explicit Memory, also known as Declarative Memory, contains the information you can consciously recall and describe. Detective 369 thinks of it as the witness testimony of the mind–the facts, events, and knowledge that you can deliberately bring to consciousness and articulate to others. This type of memory has two subcategories, each serving a different function in the detective's mental arsenal.

Episodic Memory contains the personal events of your life–your mental autobiography. Detective 369 recalls his first case, the nervous energy he felt when questioning his first suspect, the satisfaction of solving a particularly complex puzzle. These memories are tied to specific times and places, complete with sensory details and emotional context. They're like detailed case reports, each one unique and irreplaceable.

Semantic Memory, on the other hand, houses general knowledge and facts stripped of their original context. Detective 369 knows that Paris is the capital of France, that water boils at 100 degrees Celsius, and that a reliable alibi can clear a suspect–but he doesn't remember exactly when or where he learned these facts. Semantic memory is like a reference library, containing the accumulated wisdom and knowledge that informs every investigation.

The second major category is Implicit Memory, or Non-declarative Memory–the shadow evidence that influences behavior without conscious awareness. This is the memory that operates behind the scenes, like an undercover agent whose presence is felt but not seen.

Procedural Memory contains the motor skills and habits that have become second nature. Detective 369 doesn't consciously think about how to ride a bike, type on a keyboard, or draw his weapon–these skills have been encoded into his muscle memory through repetition and practice. Once learned, they operate automatically, freeing up his conscious mind for more complex tasks.

Priming and Conditioning represent the unconscious influences that shape behavior and perception. Detective 369 knows that exposure to certain stimuli can influence subsequent thoughts and actions in subtle ways. A suspect who seems nervous might prime him to look for deception, while the familiar scent of his grandfather's cologne might unconsciously influence his mood and decision-making.

Understanding these different types of memory is crucial because each requires different investigative techniques and strategies. Detective 369 has learned to work with each type's unique characteristics, using targeted methods to strengthen and enhance their effectiveness.

The Reconstruction Revelation: Memory as Creative Detective

Detective 369 pauses at his window, looking out at the city lights blinking in the darkness. One of the most important cases he ever solved was the mystery of memory itself–discovering that one of the most common misconceptions about human memory is that it works like a recording device, faithfully capturing and playing back events exactly as they occurred.

The truth, as Detective 369 discovered through careful investigation and collaboration with neuroscientists like Roediger & DeSoto, is far more fascinating and complex. Memory is reconstructive–we rebuild our memories every time we recall them. It's not like pulling a file from a cabinet and reading it exactly as it was written. Instead, it's like a skilled artist recreating a scene from fragments of sketches, photographs, and descriptions, adding details and colors that feel right based on current knowledge and emotional state.

Each reconstruction is shaped by associations, context, and emotional states. This explains why two witnesses to the same crime might remember different details, why childhood memories might shift and change over time, and why the story of a case might evolve subtly with each retelling. Detective 369 has learned to work with this reconstructive nature rather than fighting against it, using it as a tool for enhancing memory rather than lamenting its imperfections.

This reconstruction process happens seamlessly, below the threshold of consciousness. When Detective 369 recalls his first case, he's not simply retrieving a stored record–he's actively rebuilding the memory from scattered neural traces, filling in gaps with reasonable assumptions, and coloring the entire experience with his current emotional state and accumulated wisdom.

The Cold Case Files: Understanding Forgetting

Detective 369 returns to his desk and opens another file, this one labeled "Cold Cases"–the memories that have slipped away, faded, or become distorted over time. But here's what he's learned through his investigation: forgetting isn't failure. It's function. The brain, like a skilled detective, prioritizes useful or emotionally salient information while allowing less important details to fade into the background.

The reasons for forgetting are as varied as the reasons crimes go unsolved. Decay occurs when memory traces weaken over time, like footprints gradually being worn away by wind and rain. Without reinforcement, the neural pathways that encode memories become less distinct, making retrieval increasingly difficult.

Interference happens when old and new memories compete for space and attention, like trying to keep track of multiple suspects in a complex case. Sometimes new information overwrites old memories, while other times old memories make it difficult to encode new ones clearly.

Encoding failure represents cases where information was never properly stored in the first place. It's like trying to solve a case with incomplete evidence–if the initial encoding was weak or distracted, the memory may never have been properly filed away.

Retrieval failure occurs when memories exist, but the cues needed to access them are missing. Detective 369 compares this to having a case file stored somewhere in the archive but losing the filing system that would allow him to find it. The information is there, but the pathways to access it have been disrupted or forgotten.

Understanding these mechanisms of forgetting is crucial because it allows Detective 369 to work with the brain's natural tendencies rather than against them. By understanding why memories fade, he can develop strategies to strengthen the encoding process, create better retrieval cues, and build more robust memory systems.

The Investigation Manual: Your Memory Training Protocol

Detective 369 closes the case files and looks directly at you, his eyes reflecting the wisdom of years spent investigating the mysteries of the human mind. The chapters ahead will teach you how to become a detective of your own memory, equipped with techniques that have been tested in the field and proven effective in real-world situations.

You'll learn to use images, stories, and spaces to encode information with the vividness and clarity of a crime scene photograph. Visual encoding taps into the brain's natural preference for concrete, imageable information over abstract concepts. When you transform dry facts into vivid mental movies, you're working with your brain's evolutionary programming rather than against it.

You'll discover how to link new ideas to old knowledge, creating a web of associations that makes retrieval faster and more reliable. Detective 369 has learned that isolated facts are like lone suspects–hard to track and easy to lose. But when you connect new information to existing knowledge, you create a network of relationships that strengthens the entire system.

The training will show you how to store complex information in simple, repeatable systems that transform chaos into order. Like a well-organized evidence room, these systems provide structure and predictability, making it easy to file new information and retrieve it when needed.

Most importantly, you'll master the techniques of active recall and spaced repetition–the interrogation methods that ensure memories remain sharp and accessible over time. These aren't just theoretical concepts but practical tools that Detective 369 uses daily to maintain his mental acuity and investigative effectiveness.

The Case Begins

Detective 369 stands and adjusts his coat, preparing to step out into the night. But before he goes, he turns back one final time with a knowing smile. "Think of this book as a field manual for your brain," he says. We'll break down powerful techniques, show you how they work, and walk you through using them in real-life situations. You'll build a memory system that's fast, durable, and most importantly, yours.

The memory techniques you're about to learn aren't just academic exercises–they're practical tools that can transform how you learn, work, and navigate the world. Whether you're a student preparing for exams, a professional managing complex information, or simply someone who wants to remember names, faces, and important details more effectively, these methods will serve you well.

Detective 369 tips his fedora and steps toward the door, the case files tucked securely under his arm. The investigation into the nature of memory has only just begun, and already the trail is leading somewhere remarkable. In the chapters ahead, you'll discover that your brain is capable of far more than you ever imagined–you just need to learn how to work with it instead of against it.

The streetlights cast long shadows as Detective 369 disappears into the night, but his voice echoes back through the darkness: "Let's begin the investigation."

Chapter 2: Visual, Spatial, and Sequential Memory

Detective 369 stands at the threshold of a crime scene, his weathered hands adjusting the brim of his fedora as he surveys the chaos before him. The yellow tape flutters in the evening breeze, and somewhere in the distance, a siren wails its familiar song. But this isn't just any crime scene–this is the scene of a perfect crime, one that happens millions of times every day. The theft of memory itself.

The detective's keen eyes sweep across the room, taking in every detail with the practiced efficiency of someone who has learned to trust his mind's most fundamental tools. Memory, he knows, isn't just a thing–it's a scene, a layout, a journey. Our minds weren't built in sterile laboratories or quiet libraries. They were forged in ancient forests where a misremembered trail could mean death, on bustling streets where faces told stories of friend or foe, and in the endless human drama of survival and connection.

Tonight, Detective 369 is investigating the most elegant weapons in the memory detective's arsenal: the three foundational systems that anchor nearly every mnemonic technique ever devised. Visual memory, spatial memory, and sequential memory–the trinity of mental evidence that can transform any ordinary mind into an extraordinary one.

The First Witness: Visual Memory

Detective 369 kneels beside the first piece of evidence, pulling out his magnifying glass with the practiced motion of someone who has spent decades studying the intricate details that others miss. Visual memory, he reflects, is perhaps the most reliable witness in any mental investigation. It's your brain's ability to encode and recall what you see, and the research tells a remarkable story.

Standing's groundbreaking 1973 study revealed something that still amazes Detective 369 even after all these years: humans can remember thousands of images with stunning accuracy. We're not talking about perfect recall–we're talking about a recognition system so sophisticated that it puts most computer databases to shame. Show someone 10,000 pictures, and they'll recognize most of them days later. But here's the catch that every memory detective learns early in their career: this incredible ability hinges on two crucial factors–distinctiveness and association.

Detective 369 straightens up, his eyes twinkling with the kind of knowledge that comes from solving countless cases. "Picture a red fire truck," he says to himself, running through one of his favorite mental exercises. Easy enough–the image appears in his mind's eye almost instantly, clean and clear against the backdrop of his consciousness. "Now try picturing a red fire truck with a giraffe driving it and bagpipes strapped to the ladder."

The second image doesn't just appear–it explodes into existence, complete with the absurd spectacle of a spotted giraffe wearing a tiny firefighter's helmet, its long neck craned to reach the steering wheel while Scottish bagpipes wail from the ladder. The detective chuckles softly. That's the power of visual memory when you know how to work with it rather than against it.

The secret, Detective 369 has learned through years of mental investigation, lies in understanding that our brains are naturally attracted to the unusual, the exaggerated, the impossible. Mundane images fade like footprints in the rain, but bizarre, emotionally charged visuals stick like fresh paint on a suspect's hands. The more ridiculous the image, the more likely it is to survive the passage of time.

In his mental toolkit, Detective 369 carries three fundamental techniques for creating unforgettable visual evidence. First, he uses color, exaggeration, and absurdity as his primary weapons against forgetting. A simple grocery list becomes a parade of impossible images–milk cartons the size of buildings, microscopic loaves of bread, apples that glow with nuclear intensity. Second, he always imagines things in motion. Static images are like still photographs in a case file–useful, but not as compelling as the dynamic movie that plays when objects interact, collide, and transform. Third, he combines objects in bizarre ways that violate the laws of physics, logic, and common sense.

When Detective 369 needs to remember that he has a meeting with the Commissioner at 3 PM, he doesn't just write it down. He creates a mental scene where a giant clock face crashes through the Commissioner's office window, its hands pointing to 3, while the Commissioner himself juggles three burning telephones. The image is so outrageous that it's impossible to forget, and when 3 PM approaches, the mental movie plays automatically, triggering the memory with perfect timing.

The Second Witness: Spatial Memory

Detective 369 moves deeper into the crime scene, his footsteps echoing softly on the hardwood floor as he begins to map the space in his mind. Spatial memory, he knows, is the navigator of the memory world–the system that lets you remember layouts and locations with an accuracy that would make a GPS system jealous.

Every time you navigate your house in the dark, stumbling through familiar rooms without conscious thought, you're tapping into one of evolution's most sophisticated achievements. When you remember where you left your keys, when you can picture the exact location of a specific book on a crowded shelf, when you instinctively know which route will get you home fastest–that's spatial memory at work.

The detective pauses at the center of the room, closing his eyes and letting his mind build a three-dimensional map of the space. He can see every piece of furniture, every shadow, every angle where evidence might hide. This isn't magic–it's the result of specialized brain circuitry that scientists like O'Keefe & Nadel discovered in 1978. Deep in the hippocampus, networks of "place cells" fire in specific patterns, creating an internal GPS system that builds detailed mental maps of your environment.

Detective 369 opens his eyes and smiles. This spatial memory system isn't just for navigation–it's the foundation of one of the most powerful memory techniques ever developed. The Method of Loci, which he'll explore in detail later, transforms this natural ability into a tool for storing any kind of information. But even beyond formal techniques, spatial memory offers three immediate advantages for any memory detective.

First, you can build memory palaces using familiar locations. Detective 369 has mental headquarters scattered throughout the city–his childhood home for personal memories, the police station for case files, even the corner deli where he grabs his morning coffee for daily tasks and appointments. Each location becomes a storage facility for different types of information, organized and accessible whenever he needs it.

Second, you can use known locations to store abstract data. Justice becomes a blindfolded statue standing in the courthouse lobby. Democracy transforms into a voting booth positioned in the town square. Complex ideas gain concrete form when they're given specific addresses in your mental geography.

Third, you can create mental walk-throughs of information. Instead of trying to memorize a list of facts, Detective 369 creates a route that connects them spatially. The causes of World War I become stops on a walking tour through downtown, each one positioned at a specific landmark. The steps of the scientific method become a journey through the local university campus. Information that once seemed random and disconnected suddenly forms a coherent narrative path.

The detective runs his hand along the wall, feeling the texture of the paint as he demonstrates one of his favorite techniques. When he needs to remember a complex process—like the proper procedure for collecting evidence—he doesn't just memorize steps. He creates a spatial journey through the crime scene itself: step one begins at the doorway, step two moves to the victim's desk, step three occurs by the window, and so on. The physical space becomes a memory aid, with each location triggering the next action in the sequence.

The Third Witness: Sequential Memory

Detective 369 pulls out his notebook, the leather cover worn smooth by years of use, and begins to reconstruct the timeline of events. Sequential memory, he knows, is the chronicler of the memory world–the system that keeps track of order, sequence, and the crucial progression of time.

Some memories, the detective reflects as he flips through pages of careful notes, depend entirely on getting the order right. A phone number becomes useless if you transpose the digits. A recipe fails if you add ingredients in the wrong sequence. A criminal's alibi falls apart if the timing doesn't match the evidence. Sequential memory is your mind's ability to hold items in a specific order, and it's especially crucial for the kind of systematic thinking that solves cases.

In his long career, Detective 369 has found sequential memory indispensable for four types of mental evidence. Routines form the backbone of effective detective work–the systematic approach to questioning witnesses, the methodical process of analyzing evidence, the careful sequence of steps that ensures nothing important is overlooked. Steps in a process must be followed precisely, whether you're developing photographs in the darkroom or reconstructing a crime scene. Historical timelines help establish context and causation–understanding not just what happened, but when it happened and how events influenced each other. And speech outlines ensure that when Detective 369 testifies in court, his testimony flows logically from one point to the next, building a compelling case that judges and juries can follow.

The detective has developed three primary techniques for strengthening sequential memory. First, he uses rhyme, rhythm, and narrative flow to create natural progressions that the mind wants to follow. Information that flows like a song or story resists the chaos of forgetting. Second, he builds image chains using the linking method–each item in a sequence becomes a vivid mental image that connects to the next one in an impossible but unforgettable way. Third, he numbers his pegs and locations, creating a systematic framework that can accommodate any sequence of any length.

When Detective 369 needs to remember the Bill of Rights in order, he doesn't just read them repeatedly. He creates a mental journey through a courthouse where each amendment is represented by a dramatic scene at a numbered location. The First Amendment becomes a passionate speaker standing on a soapbox at location one, the Second Amendment transforms into a museum display case at location two, and so on. The sequence becomes a story, and the story becomes unforgettable.

The Perfect Crime: Combining All Three Systems

Detective 369 closes his notebook and looks up at the crime scene with new eyes. The real breakthrough in memory investigation, he knows, comes when you realize that you don't have to choose between visual, spatial, and sequential memory systems. The most elegant solutions combine all three, creating a mental framework so robust that forgetting becomes nearly impossible.

The detective demonstrates this principle with one of his favorite examples. Imagine you need to memorize a 10-point checklist for investigating a burglary. Using only traditional methods, you might write it down, read it repeatedly, and hope for the best. But Detective 369 approaches it like the master investigator he is.

First, he turns each point into a vivid image, engaging his visual memory system. "Check for signs of forced entry" becomes a crowbar with glowing red eyes, breathing steam in the cold night air. "Interview witnesses" transforms into a giant ear sprouting legs, chasing after a group of terrified bystanders.

"Collect fingerprints" becomes a massive magnifying glass that hovers in the air, dropping glowing fingerprints like snow.

Next, he places each image in a room of his mental headquarters, engaging his spatial memory system. The crowbar appears at the front door, the giant ear in the living room, the magnifying glass in the kitchen. Each location is distinct and memorable, providing a concrete address for each abstract concept.

Finally, he walks through the rooms in order, engaging his sequential memory system. The investigation becomes a tour through familiar space, with each room revealing the next step in the process. The spatial journey ensures that the sequence is preserved, while the vivid images ensure that each step is unforgettable.

The result is memory magic. What began as a dry checklist has become a mental movie, complete with settings, characters, and plot. Detective 369 isn't just memorizing–he's experiencing the memory. The information doesn't just exist in his mind–it lives there, breathing and dynamic and ready to be accessed whenever he needs it.

The Investigation Continues

Detective 369 steps back from the crime scene, his investigation complete. The evidence is clear: visual, spatial, and sequential memory systems don't just store information–they transform it. They take the abstract and make it concrete, the forgettable and make it unforgettable, the chaotic and make it ordered.

By the end of this investigation, the detective knows, you'll understand how to use these systems fluently, often in combination, to track any idea, sequence, or system. Visual memory will help you create images so vivid they refuse to fade. Spatial memory will provide the architecture to house your mental treasures. Sequential memory will preserve the order and flow that turns random facts into coherent knowledge.

The detective adjusts his fedora one final time and heads toward the exit, his footsteps confident and purposeful. The crime scene of forgotten memories has been solved, the evidence collected and cataloged. Visual, spatial, sequential–the trinity of memory systems that can transform any mind into a precision instrument of recall.

The fog rolls in from the harbor as Detective 369 disappears into the night, but his voice echoes back through the darkness: "Your mental scene of the crime just got clearer. The investigation continues."

Chapter 3: Core Memory Principles

Detective 369 sits at his desk in the pre-dawn darkness, three case files spread before him like a hand of cards. The amber glow of his desk lamp illuminates photographs, witness statements, and evidence markers–the scattered pieces of three different investigations that have consumed his nights for weeks. But tonight, something clicks. As he studies the files, patterns emerge from the chaos. Connections form between seemingly unrelated clues. The fog of confusion lifts, revealing the elegant architecture beneath.

Every great detective knows that memorization relies on three fundamental strategies that transform chaos into clarity, confusion into comprehension. These aren't just techniques–they're the operating principles that make the difference between a case that goes cold and one that cracks wide open. In every investigation, whether you're tracking a suspect through the labyrinthine streets of the city or tracking an idea through the labyrinthine corridors of your mind, you need a few essential tools: follow the connections, simplify the chaos, and revisit the scene.

Your memory operates on these same principles. The techniques that fill the pages of this book–the linking methods, the memory palaces, the peg systems–are all built on three core strategies that Detective 369 has refined through decades of mental investigation. Master these three principles, and every memory system becomes easier to learn and faster to use. They are the foundation upon which all memory mastery is built, the frame that gives structure to the techniques that follow.

Tonight, Detective 369 opens these three essential case files, each one containing the secrets that separate the amateurs from the professionals, the forgetful from the unforgettable.

The First Strategy: Association - Following the Connections

Detective 369 picks up the first file, its tab marked "ASSOCIATIONS" in his careful handwriting. Inside are dozens of photographs connected by red string, creating a web of relationships that would look like madness to an outsider but represents perfect clarity to the trained investigative mind. This is the visual representation of memory's most fundamental truth: memory is not about data–it's about relationships.

When you remember something, Detective 369 explains as he traces the connections with his finger, you're not retrieving isolated facts from some mental filing cabinet. You're recalling what that information is connected to, what it relates to, what it reminds you of. Memory is an associative network; a living web of connections that grows stronger and more complex with each new link you forge.

Consider this scenario: you meet someone named Rose at a crowded party. Alone, that's just a name floating in the social static of introductions and handshakes. But if you imagine a rose blooming out of her hair, its petals unfurling as she speaks, you've connected that abstract name to something familiar and memorable. The visual image creates a bridge between the new information and your existing knowledge, transforming a forgettable encounter into an unforgettable one.

This isn't just Detective 369's intuition–it's the foundation of how memory works. Association is one of the most fundamental mechanisms of memory, documented by researchers like Bower as early as 1970. Semantic networks, schemas, and story-based encoding all rely on this principle. When you create mnemonics, when you use the keyword method, when you build linking systems, you're harnessing the brain's natural tendency to create connections between ideas.

Detective 369 demonstrates this with one of his favorite examples. He needs to remember that the suspect in the Anderson case drives a blue Toyota Camry. Rather than simply repeating "blue Toyota Camry" until it sticks, he creates a vivid association: he imagines Anderson himself painted entirely blue, cramming his oversized frame into a toy car so small his knees are pressed against his chin. The image is ridiculous, impossible, and therefore unforgettable. The connection between Anderson and his vehicle is now cemented in Detective 369's mind through the power of association.

The strength of association lies in its multiplication effect. Each new connection doesn't just help you remember one piece of information–it strengthens the entire network. When Detective 369 later learns that Anderson works at a paint store, the blue imagery becomes even more vivid and memorable. The paint store connects to the blue color, which connects to the toy car, which connects to Anderson himself. The web of associations grows stronger with each new thread.

Detective 369 has learned to spot the different types of associations that make memory work. Semantic associations connect ideas through meaning–doctor links to hospital, storm links to lightning, happiness links to sunshine. These are the obvious connections, the ones that feel natural and logical. But phonetic associations, connecting ideas through similar sounds, can be even more powerful for memory work. The name "Campbell" becomes a camel with a bell, "Belarus" becomes a bear with a lasso, "photosynthesis" becomes a photo of a thesis.

Visual associations transform abstract concepts into concrete images. Justice becomes a blindfolded figure holding scales, democracy becomes a voting booth, infinity becomes a sideways eight floating in space. Emotional associations link information to feelings–the pride of solving a difficult case, the frustration of a dead-end lead, the satisfaction of a puzzle piece clicking into place. The stronger the emotional connection, the more durable the memory.

Detective 369 closes the first file with satisfaction. Association is the foundation of all memory work, the principle that transforms isolated facts into interconnected knowledge. Without it, information remains scattered and fragile. With it, every piece of data becomes part of a larger, more resilient structure.

The Second Strategy: Chunking - Simplifying the Chaos

The second file bears the label "CHUNKING" in Detective 369's methodical script. As he opens it, he reveals a different kind of organization–not the web of connections from the first file, but a series of neat groupings, information sorted into manageable clusters that the mind can handle with ease.

Detective 369 knows that even the most capable investigator has limits. Your working memory, that mental space where you actively process information, can only handle so much at once. George Miller's famous research, published in 1956, put the limit at seven items, plus or minus two–what psychologists call "Miller's Magic Number". Try to juggle more than that, and important details start slipping through the cracks.

But Detective 369 has discovered a solution that every great investigator learns: chunking. By grouping information into larger, more meaningful units, you can dramatically expand your mental capacity. It's not about changing the limits of your mind–it's about working smarter within those limits.

He demonstrates with a phone number that arrived in an anonymous tip: 8002748273. Presented as a string of ten individual digits, it pushes your working memory to its breaking point. But Detective 369 doesn't see ten separate numbers. He sees three chunks: 800-274-8273. Suddenly, ten items become three, comfortably within the range of what your mind can handle effortlessly.

The transformation is remarkable. What seemed like an impossible string of digits becomes a manageable piece of information. The first chunk, 800, signals a toll-free number. The second chunk, 274, might connect to a specific area or service. The third chunk, 8273, provides the unique identifier. Each chunk carries meaning, and meaning makes memory stick.

Detective 369 has found that chunking works across all types of information. Numbers group into years, codes, or significant dates. The digits 1776 aren't just four separate numbers–they're a single chunk representing American independence. The sequence 911 isn't nine-one-one–it's an emergency code that carries instant recognition and emotional weight.

Words transform into acronyms or keywords that capture entire concepts. Instead of remembering "Federal Bureau of Investigation," you chunk it into "FBI." Instead of memorizing "As Soon As Possible," you chunk it into "ASAP." The individual letters become meaningless; the chunk carries the full meaning.

Images combine several ideas into one mental picture. Detective 369 needs to remember that the suspect is tall, wearing a red coat, and carrying a briefcase. Rather than holding three separate pieces of information in his mind, he creates a single chunked image: a towering figure in a crimson coat, the briefcase swinging at his side like a pendulum as he walks. Three details become one vivid picture.

The real power of chunking emerges when you combine it with association. Detective 369 demonstrates this with a case involving multiple suspects. Rather than trying to remember each person's individual characteristics, he groups them by their roles: the mastermind, the muscle, and the inside man. Each group becomes a chunk, and within each chunk, he uses association to link the specific details. The mastermind wears glasses that reflect dollar signs. The muscle has arms like tree trunks. The inside man carries keys that jingle like wind chimes.

Detective 369 has learned that effective chunking requires finding the right level of grouping. Too small, and you're not really simplifying the information. Too large, and the chunks become unwieldy and hard to remember. The art lies in finding the natural boundaries, the places where information logically groups together.

Subject matter often provides natural chunking opportunities. Historical events group by time, scientific concepts group by field of study, and foreign vocabulary groups by theme or grammatical structure. Detective 369 remembers the Bill of Rights not as ten separate amendments, but as four coherent chunks: fundamental freedoms (Amendments 1-3), criminal justice rights (4-6), civil trial rules (7-8), and constitutional structure (9-10). The grouping makes the information more manageable and reveals the logical organization beneath the surface.

Sometimes, Detective 369 creates artificial chunks when natural ones don't exist. A random list of evidence items becomes grouped by location where they were found, by size, by material, or by relevance to the case. The specific grouping matters less than the act of grouping itself–the mind craves organization and rewards you with better recall when you provide it.

As Detective 369 closes the second file, he reflects on the power of chunking to transform overwhelming information into manageable knowledge. It's not about memorizing more–it's about organizing better. When you chunk effectively, you're not just remembering information; you're understanding its structure and relationships.

The Third Strategy: Active Recall - Revisiting the Scene

The third file is thicker than the others, its pages worn from frequent consultation. The tab reads "ACTIVE RECALL" in letters that seem to pulse with energy. Detective 369 opens it with the reverence of someone who knows he's about to reveal the most powerful weapon in his investigative arsenal.

Most people, Detective 369 explains as he settles back in his chair, study the way they investigate–passively. They reread old files, review the same evidence repeatedly, flip through photographs hoping something will stick. It's the equivalent of standing at a crime scene and staring at the same footprint repeatedly, hoping it will somehow become more meaningful with repetition.

But Detective 369 has learned that the mind, like any good investigator, gets sharp with questioning. Not by passively reviewing old files, but by actively asking, digging, and pulling answers from the depths of consciousness. This is Active Recall—the practice of testing yourself rather than simply reviewing material.

The difference is profound. When you reread your notes, you're giving your brain the illusion of knowledge. The information feels familiar, so you assume you know it. But familiarity is not the same as recall. It's the difference between recognizing a suspect in a lineup and being able to describe them from memory. Recognition is passive; recall is active.

Active Recall works because retrieval is learning. Each time you force your brain to pull information from memory, you're strengthening the neural pathways that store that information. It's like solving a case repeatedly–each time you work through the evidence, the connections become clearer, the conclusions more automatic, the entire investigation more efficient.

Detective 369 demonstrates this with a simple exercise. He reads a paragraph from a case file, then closes it and asks himself: "What were the three main pieces of evidence? How did the timeline unfold? What connections did I notice?" He doesn't peek at the notes. He doesn't give himself hints. He digs into his memory and pulls out what he can remember, even if it's incomplete or imperfect.

The struggle is the point. Research by Roediger & Karpicke has shown that the more effortful the retrieval, the deeper the memory imprint becomes. When you must work to remember something, your brain treats it as important information worth preserving. When information comes easily, your brain assumes it's not worth the metabolic cost of strong encoding.

Detective 369 has developed several techniques for implementing Active Recall in his daily work. The simplest is the "blank page method"–after reviewing a case file, he takes out a blank sheet of paper and writes down everything he can remember without looking back at the original. The gaps in his knowledge become immediately apparent, showing him exactly what needs more attention.

He uses flashcards for key facts, suspects' descriptions, and legal procedures. But these aren't ordinary flashcards–they're questions that force him to think, to analyze, to connect information. Instead of "What is the Fourth Amendment?" he asks, "In what situations would the Fourth Amendment be relevant to this case?" The difference transforms passive recognition into active analysis.

Detective 369 also uses the "explain it to someone else" method. He imagines teaching a rookie detective about the case, forcing himself to articulate not just what happened, but why it matters, how the pieces fit together, what conclusions can be drawn. The act of explanation reveals gaps in understanding that simple review never exposes.

The timing of Active Recall is crucial. Detective 369 has learned that testing yourself immediately after learning something is helpful but testing yourself just as you're about to forget is transformative. This is where Active Recall connects to the broader science of memory–the optimal timing that psychologists call "spaced repetition."

Memory isn't just about the questions you ask–it's about when you ask them. Recalling something once helps. Recalling it again, just as it's beginning to fade, creates a memory that's stronger than the original. Detective 369 schedules his reviews strategically: he tests himself on new information after one day, then after three days, then after a week, then after two weeks. Each review interrupts the natural forgetting process just in time, reinforcing the memory before it slips away.

This isn't just theory–it's practice that Detective 369 has refined through years of investigation. He's learned that consistency matters more than intensity. Better to spend fifteen minutes daily testing yourself than to spend three hours weekly rereading notes. The brain responds to regular challenge, not sporadic cramming.

Detective 369 has also discovered that failed recall is almost as valuable as successful recall. When he can't remember something, he doesn't just look up the answer–he analyzes why he forgot it. Was the association too weak? Did he fail to chunk the information properly? Was the original encoding insufficient? Each failure becomes a learning opportunity, a chance to strengthen the memory system itself.

As Detective 369 closes the third file, he reflects on the power of Active Recall to transform passive knowledge into active expertise. It's not about studying harder–it's about studying smarter. When you test yourself regularly, you're not just memorizing information; you're building the mental muscle that makes all future learning easier.

The Perfect Investigation: How the Three Strategies Work Together

Detective 369 leans back in his chair, the three files now arranged in a neat row before him. Association, Chunking, Active Recall-the trinity of memory principles that transform ordinary minds into extraordinary ones. But the real power, he knows, comes not from using these strategies in isolation, but from combining them into a comprehensive approach that leverages all three simultaneously.

He demonstrates this with a case that has challenged him for weeks: memorizing the Bill of Rights in order. Using traditional methods-reading and rereading the amendments-he might eventually achieve a fragile, temporary familiarity. But Detective 369 approaches it like the skilled investigator he is, deploying all three strategies in coordination.

First, he uses Association to transform each amendment into a vivid mental image. The First Amendment becomes a passionate speaker standing on a soapbox, his voice carrying the power of free speech across a crowded square. The Second Amendment transforms into a museum display case containing historical weapons, representing the right to bear arms. The Third Amendment becomes a homeowner slamming the door in the face of a soldier trying to force his way in, protecting the right against forced quartering.

Each image is bizarre, emotional, and impossible to ignore. Detective 369 doesn't just create pictures-he creates movies, complete with action, sound, and sensory details. The more absurd the associations, the more memorable they become.

Next, he applies Chunking to organize the ten amendments into manageable groups. The first three amendments deal with fundamental freedoms-speech, arms, and quartering. The next three focus on criminal justice-searches, due process, and trial rights. The seventh and eighth amendments address civil courts and cruel punishment. The final two amendments deal with constitutional structure-reserved powers and federalism.

By grouping the amendments thematically, Detective 369 transforms ten separate items into four coherent chunks. The organizational structure provides a logical framework that makes the sequence easier to remember and understand. He's not just memorizing a list–he's learning the architecture of constitutional rights.

Finally, he implements Active Recall to cement the information in long-term memory. Instead of simply reviewing the amendments, he tests himself repeatedly. He starts with the basic sequence: "What are the first three amendments?" Then he moves to deeper questions: "How do the Fourth and Fifth Amendments work together?" "What's the difference between the Seventh and Eighth Amendments?" "How do the Ninth and Tenth Amendments balance federal and state power?"

He schedules these self-tests strategically, using spaced repetition to maximize retention. Day one: test immediately after initial learning. Day three: test again as the memory begins to fade. Day seven: test once more to reinforce the weakening traces. Day fourteen: final test to ensure long-term retention.

The result is memory magic. What began as a dry constitutional lesson becomes a vivid mental drama, organized into logical chapters, and reinforced through active engagement. Detective 369 doesn't just know the Bill of Rights–he experiences it. The information doesn't just exist in his mind–it lives there, breathing and dynamic and ready to be accessed whenever needed.

This integrated approach works because it mirrors how the brain naturally processes information. Association creates the connections that make information meaningful. Chunking provides the organization that makes information manageable. Active Recall supplies the reinforcement that makes information permanent.

Detective 369 has used this triple strategy to master everything from legal precedents to forensic procedures, from suspect descriptions to courtroom protocols. The specific content changes, but the approach remains constant: connect, organize, and test. Make it meaningful, make it manageable, make it memorable.

The Foundation of All Memory Work

Detective 369 stands and walks to his window, looking out at the city lights that sparkle in the darkness like neural connections in the vast network of the mind. The three files behind him represent more than techniques–they're the fundamental principles that underlie every memory system ever devised.

These three strategies aren't just the foundation of memory work–they're the frame that gives structure to everything that follows. When Detective 369 teaches the Linking Method in the next chapter, he's showing you how to use Association to create connections between items. When he reveals the secrets of the Memory Palace, he's demonstrating how to use Chunking to organize information spatially. When he explains the power of spaced repetition, he's showing you how to use Active Recall to make memories permanent.

Every mnemonic technique, every memory system, every cognitive strategy builds on these three principles. Master them, and every new method will snap into place like a puzzle piece finding its natural position. Neglect them, and even the most sophisticated techniques will remain fragile and unreliable.

Detective 369 returns to his desk and gathers the three files, stacking them neatly in order of importance. Association first–the foundation of all memory work. Chunking second–the organization that makes information manageable. Active Recall third–the reinforcement that makes memories permanent.

These aren't just abstract concepts–they're practical tools that you can start using immediately. Don't wait for the advanced techniques. Don't postpone practice until you've read the entire book. Start now, tonight, with the information you need to remember today.

Take whatever you're trying to learn and ask yourself: What can I connect this to? How can I organize this information? How can I test myself on this material? The answers will guide you toward more effective learning, stronger memory, and deeper understanding.

The fog outside Detective 369's window begins to lift as dawn approaches, revealing the clear outline of the city below. Similarly, the fog of confusion that surrounds memory work begins to clear when you understand these fundamental principles. Association, Chunking, Active Recall–the three strategies that transform chaos into clarity, confusion into comprehension.

Detective 369 adjusts his fedora and prepares to step into the morning light. The foundational cases are closed, the principles established, the stage set for the techniques that follow. Association has shown you how to follow the connections. Chunking has taught you how to simplify the chaos. Active Recall has revealed the power of revisiting the scene.

The investigation into memory mastery is well underway. The tools are in your hands, the strategies are in your mind, and the techniques that follow will build upon this solid foundation. Detective 369 tips his hat in satisfaction—another successful investigation, another mystery solved, another step toward mastery of the most important skill of all: the art of remembering.

Chapter 4: Linking and Substitute Word Method

Detective 369 sits at his desk in the dim glow of his desk lamp, a chain of evidence spread before him like a silver necklace gleaming in the darkness. Each link connects to the next with perfect precision, creating an unbreakable sequence that tells the story of a solved case. Tonight, he's about to reveal two of the most elegant weapons in the memory detective's arsenal: the Linking Method and the Substitute Word Method. These aren't just techniques–they're the art of creating mental chains so strong that forgetting becomes impossible.

In every great investigation, Detective 369 knows, one clue leads to another. The smallest detail–a footprint in the mud, a thread caught on a fence, a witness's half-remembered face–becomes the first link in a chain that eventually leads to the truth. Memory works the same way. Information that seems impossible to remember becomes effortless when you create the right connections, forging mental links that guide your mind from one piece of evidence to the next.

The Linking Method is the foundation of this mental detective work. It transforms any list, any sequence, any collection of facts into a vivid story where each element naturally leads to the next. Combined with the Substitute Word Method–the technique that turns abstract concepts into concrete images–these two approaches become a powerful partnership for conquering even the most challenging information.

Detective 369 has used these methods to memorize everything from witness statements to complex legal procedures, from suspect descriptions to intricate case timelines. Tonight, he's going to show you how to build your own chains of evidence, creating mental movies so compelling that your brain will replay them automatically whenever you need to recall the information.

The First Link: Understanding the Linking Method

Detective 369 stands and walks to his evidence board, where dozens of photographs are connected by red string in a complex web of relationships. Each image tells part of the story, but it's the connections between them that reveal the complete truth. The Linking Method works on the same principle, turning separate pieces of information into a connected narrative that the mind can follow effortlessly.

At its core, the Linking Method is elegantly simple. You take each item you want to remember and transform it into a vivid mental image. Then you create bizarre, impossible, emotionally charged connections between these images, building a chain where each image naturally triggers the memory of the next one. The result is a mental movie that plays automatically in your mind, with each scene leading inevitably to the next.

The power of this technique lies in how it leverages the brain's natural associative networks. Research by cognitive psychologists like Allan Paivio has shown that our minds are extraordinarily good at remembering visual information, especially when it's connected to other images through meaningful relationships. The Linking Method doesn't fight against your brain's natural tendencies–it harnesses them, turning the chaos of disconnected facts into the ordered beauty of a well-constructed story.

Detective 369 demonstrates this with a simple example. Imagine you need to remember a grocery list: milk, hammer, grapes, and soap. Presented as a list, these items have no natural connection. Your brain struggles to find the thread that ties them together. But Detective 369 doesn't see a list–he sees the beginning of a case.

The story begins with a giant milk carton, tall as a building, teetering precariously on the edge of a skyscraper. Without warning, it tips over and crashes down with tremendous force, its contents exploding across the city street below. From the chaos emerges Detective 369 himself, soaked in milk and reaching for his weapon–but instead of his usual revolver, he finds a massive hammer in his holster, its handle slick with the white liquid.

He swings the hammer with all his strength, but instead of striking a suspect, it smashes into an enormous cluster of grapes that appears suddenly in front of him. The grapes burst like tiny water balloons, sending purple juice cascading everywhere. The juice flows toward a storm drain, but as it approaches the opening, the drain suddenly erupts with a geyser of sudsy soap, the bubbles rising like a fountain of foam that blankets the entire scene.

Each element of the story connects to the next through impossible but unforgettable action. The milk leads to the hammer, the hammer leads to the grapes, the grapes lead to the soap. The more ridiculous the connections, the more memorable they become. Detective 369 has learned that the brain pays attention to the unusual, the exaggerated, the impossible. Mundane images fade like footprints in the rain, but bizarre visuals stick like evidence at a crime scene.

This isn't just intuition–it's science. The method works because it engages multiple memory systems simultaneously. The visual imagery activates the brain's powerful image-processing networks. The narrative structure engages sequential memory, creating a natural flow from one element to the next. The emotional content–the surprise, the absurdity, the impossible physics–triggers the amygdala, which enhances memory consolidation. Most importantly, the bizarre associations create distinctive, unique memory traces that are difficult to confuse with other information.

The Art of Creating Unforgettable Links

Detective 369 returns to his desk and opens a thick manual titled "The Four Rules of Mental Evidence." These aren't just guidelines–they're the fundamental principles that transform ordinary images into extraordinary memories. Every memory detective learns these rules early in their training, and Detective 369 has refined them through years of fieldwork.

1. Proportion Distortion: In the real world, objects maintain predictable relationships to each other. A milk carton is smaller than a hammer, which is smaller than a person. But in the memory detective's world, these relationships are weapons to be wielded. Make things impossibly large or impossibly small. Picture a microscopic hammer trying to crack a giant grape the size of a house. Imagine a milk carton so tiny it fits in your pocket yet somehow contains enough liquid to flood an entire city block. The brain notices these violations of natural law and files them away as significant events.

2. Numerical Exaggeration: Instead of one of something, picture thousands. Instead of a few, imagine millions. If grapes are part of your chain, don't settle for a small bunch—envision an avalanche of grapes pouring from the sky, each one the size of a bowling ball, bouncing and rolling through the streets like a purple tsunami. The sheer scale of the impossible creates a memory that refuses to fade.

3. Violent Action: This doesn't mean gruesome or disturbing imagery—it means dynamic, energetic, impossible physics. Things crash, explode, penetrate, collide, and transform. The milk carton doesn't just fall—it plummets like a meteor, leaving a crater in the pavement. The hammer doesn't just hit—

it smashes through the grapes with the force of a thunderbolt, sending juice flying in all directions. The soap doesn't just appear—it erupts like a volcano, coating everything in sight with bubbles that sparkle like diamonds.

4. Substitution and Transformation: Don't just use the literal objects—let them become something else, something unexpected but related. The milk carton becomes a cow that moos musically as it falls. The hammer transforms into a judge's gavel that pounds with the rhythm of a heartbeat. The grapes become tiny balloons that pop with the sound of laughter. The soap becomes a cloud that rains bubbles instead of water.

Detective 369 has discovered that these rules work because they create what memory researchers call "elaborative encoding." Instead of simply trying to memorize the word "milk," you're creating a rich, multi-sensory experience that involves sight, sound, motion, emotion, and meaning. The brain doesn't just store the word–it stores the entire experience. When you need to recall the list, you don't just remember "milk"–you remember the spectacular crash, the impossible physics, the vivid colors, and the emotional impact of the scene.

The Second Weapon: The Substitute Word Method

Detective 369 opens a second file, this one labeled "Witness Protection Program." Inside are dozens of photographs, each showing the same person with different appearances–different hair, different clothes, different expressions. This is the visual metaphor for the Substitute Word Method: taking something abstract, foreign, or difficult to visualize and giving it a concrete, memorable identity.

The Substitute Word Method tackles one of memory's most persistent challenges: how to remember information that doesn't naturally lend itself to visual imagery. Abstract concepts, foreign words, technical terms, proper names–these are the suspects that slip through the cracks of ordinary memory systems. They're too vague, too unfamiliar, or too complex to form vivid mental images. But Detective 369 has learned to give these elusive suspects new identities, transforming them into concrete, visual forms that the mind can easily capture and hold.

The technique works through phonetic similarity and visual association. Any word, no matter how abstract or foreign, is fundamentally a collection of sounds. The Substitute Word Method finds familiar words or phrases that sound like the target information, then creates vivid mental images that connect these substitute sounds to the meaning you need to remember. It's like creating a witness protection program for difficult information–giving it a new identity that's easier to recognize and remember.

Detective 369 demonstrates this with a challenging example from his forensics training. The term "mitochondria"–the cellular powerhouses that generate energy in every cell–is notoriously difficult to remember. It's abstract, scientific, and doesn't naturally suggest any visual imagery. But Detective 369 doesn't see "mitochondria"–he hears "mighty cone dry ya."

The substitute phrase leads to a vivid mental image: a mighty, massive traffic cone standing in the middle of a busy intersection, its orange surface gleaming in the sunlight. But this isn't an ordinary cone–it's a magical device that has the power to dry anything it touches. Cars drive through its shadow and emerge completely dried; their wet surfaces instantly transformed to pristine condition. The cone radiates energy, sending waves of drying power in all directions.

The image connects the sound "mighty cone dry ya" to the meaning "cellular powerhouse that generates energy." The cone's drying power represents the mitochondria's energy-generating function. The mighty, impressive nature of the cone reflects the critical importance of mitochondria in cellular function. The visual is so striking, so impossible, that it becomes unforgettable.

This isn't just wordplay–it's neuroscience in action. The Substitute Word Method works because it creates what researchers call "dual coding"–information that's stored in both verbal and visual memory systems. The phonetic similarity provides the verbal bridge, while the vivid imagery provides the visual anchor. When you need to recall "mitochondria," the substitute sounds trigger the visual image, and the visual image triggers the meaning.

Detective 369 has used this technique to master everything from foreign languages to legal terminology. French words become English sounds with visual bridges. Legal concepts become concrete images with emotional connections. Scientific terms become familiar objects with impossible powers. Each substitute word acts as an undercover agent, infiltrating the suspect's identity and making it accessible to memory.

Building Complex Chains: The Partnership in Action

Detective 369 pulls out a case file marked "Planetary Investigation"–a complex case involving multiple suspects in a specific sequence. This is where the Linking Method and Substitute Word Method join forces, creating an investigative partnership that can handle even the most challenging information. The case involves memorizing the planets in order from the sun: Mercury, Venus, Earth, Mars, Jupiter, Saturn, Uranus, Neptune.

Some of these suspects are easy to visualize—Earth, Mars, and Saturn with its distinctive rings. But others, like Mercury and Uranus, present challenges. Mercury is just a name, difficult to transform into memorable imagery. Uranus is awkward to pronounce and even more awkward to visualize. This is where the partnership between linking and substitution becomes crucial.

Detective 369 begins his investigation with Mercury, using the Substitute Word Method to transform the abstract name into concrete imagery. "Mercury" becomes "Mercury"–not the planet, but the liquid metal that flows like silver water. In his mind, he sees a massive thermometer, its silver Mercury contents glowing with inner light. The thermometer is so large it dwarfs buildings, and its Mercury contents are cascading out like a waterfall of liquid silver.

The silver cascade flows directly onto the next suspect: Venus. But Venus isn't just a planet–she's a goddess, beautiful and radiant, wearing a crown of molten lava that pulses with volcanic energy. The liquid Mercury from the thermometer doesn't harm her–instead, it forms a shimmering silver dress that flows around her like liquid starlight. She stands on a pedestal of gleaming metal, her hands outstretched as if blessing the scene.

Venus doesn't just stand there–she acts. With a gesture of cosmic power, she hurls a massive projectile through space. The projectile is Earth itself, spinning like a top and glowing with blue-green light. But this isn't a gentle toss–Earth crashes with tremendous force, splitting open like a cosmic egg. The impact is so violent that the planet's crust cracks and separates, revealing its molten core.

From the fiery yolk of the broken Earth emerges the next suspect: Mars. But Mars isn't just a red planet–he's a Roman god of war, fully armored and riding a chariot made of rust-red metal. His armor gleams with the color of dried blood, and his chariot is pulled by horses that breathe fire instead of air. Mars raises his spear–a weapon so massive it could pierce moons–and hurls it with all his divine strength.

The spear flies through space and strikes the next target: Jupiter. But Jupiter isn't just a gas giant–it's an enormous balloon, striped with swirling colors and floating in the void like a cosmic carnival decoration. The spear doesn't just hit the balloon–it pierces it completely, causing Jupiter to explode in a spectacular burst of gas and color. The explosion is so powerful that it creates a rain of debris that falls like confetti across the solar system.

The debris doesn't fall randomly–it forms the rings of Saturn. But Saturn isn't just a ringed planet–it's a cosmic juggler, spinning multiple rings around its body like a performer in a celestial circus. The rings glow with ice and rock, creating a beautiful but impossible display of physics-defying artistry. Saturn catches one of its rings and, with a practiced motion, tosses it like a frisbee toward the next target.

The ring spins through space and strikes Uranus. But Detective 369 has solved the pronunciation problem through substitution–"Uranus" becomes "Your-anus," which becomes "your-a-nus," which becomes "your-a-moose." In his mind, he sees a massive, majestic moose standing in the depths of space, its antlers covered with ice crystals that sparkle like diamonds. The moose is so cold that its breath creates frozen clouds, and its fur is the color of deep space itself.

The ring from Saturn doesn't just hit the moose–it circles around its neck like a cosmic collar. The moose, now decorated with Saturn's ring, rears up on its hind legs and kicks with tremendous force. The kick is so powerful that it creates a tidal wave in space itself, a wave of cosmic energy that rushes toward the final suspect.

The wave strikes Neptune, but Neptune isn't just a distant planet–he's the Roman god of the sea, rising from cosmic waters with a trident that crackles with electrical energy. His beard flows with liquid starlight, and his eyes hold the deep blue of interstellar space. Neptune doesn't just stand in the wave–he surfs it, riding the cosmic tsunami with the skill of a deity who has mastered the forces of the universe.

The entire chain becomes a cosmic crime story, with each suspect leading inevitably to the next through impossible but unforgettable action. Mercury's liquid silver flows onto Venus, Venus hurls Earth, Earth cracks to reveal Mars, Mars spears Jupiter, Jupiter explodes to create Saturn's rings, Saturn tosses a ring to the space moose, and the moose kicks a wave that Neptune surfs to the edge of the solar system.

The Science Behind the Chain

Detective 369 closes the planetary case file and opens a thick research manual titled "Neurological Evidence." The techniques he's demonstrated aren't just creative exercises–they're applications of decades of memory research, refined through scientific investigation and proven effective in countless studies.

The Linking Method works because it creates what neuroscientists call "elaborative rehearsal." Instead of simply repeating information, you're creating rich, multi-dimensional experiences that engage multiple areas of the brain. The visual imagery activates the occipital lobe, the region responsible for processing visual information. The narrative structure engages the prefrontal cortex, which handles sequential reasoning and story comprehension. The emotional content–the surprise, humor, and absurdity–triggers the amygdala, which enhances memory consolidation by marking the information as significant.

Research by cognitive psychologist Allan Paivio has shown that information stored in both verbal and visual formats is significantly easier to recall than information stored in only one format. This "dual coding theory" explains why the combination of linking and substitution is so effective. The linking provides the visual narrative, while the substitution provides the verbal bridge. Together, they create memories that are encoded in multiple formats, making them more resilient and easier to retrieve.

The bizarre nature of the imagery isn't just for entertainment–it's a fundamental requirement for effective memory encoding. The brain has evolved to notice and remember unusual events because they're more likely to be significant for survival. This is why Detective 369 emphasizes impossible physics, exaggerated proportions, and violent action. These elements trigger what psychologists call the "bizarreness effect"–the phenomenon where unusual information is remembered better than ordinary information.

The method also leverages the brain's natural tendency toward "clustering" and "chunking." Instead of trying to remember individual items, you're creating meaningful groups connected by logical relationships. The planets become a single story with multiple chapters. The grocery list becomes a unified crime scene with multiple pieces of evidence. This organization makes the information easier to process and dramatically improves recall accuracy.

Applications for Every Detective

Detective 369 walks to his filing cabinet and pulls out three folders labeled "Student," "Professional," and "Lifelong Learner." Each folder contains dozens of case studies showing how the linking and substitution methods can be adapted to different types of information and different learning contexts.

The Student Detective

For students, these techniques transform the challenge of academic memorization into an engaging creative exercise. Detective 369 opens the first folder and reveals a case study from his work with a history student struggling to memorize the causes of World War I. The traditional approach–reading and rereading lists of causes–had failed completely. But by applying linking and substitution, the student transformed abstract historical concepts into an unforgettable narrative.

The story begins with "Militarism," which becomes "Military-ism"–a giant military tank covered in medals and flags, rolling through the streets of early 20th-century Europe. The tank doesn't just drive–it crashes directly into a massive spider web that stretches between buildings. This web represents "Alliance systems," transformed into a literal web of sticky silk that traps everything it touches.

The tank's collision with the web creates vibrations that wake up a sleeping giant–"Imperialism" becomes "Imperial-ism," visualized as a massive emperor wearing a crown made of world maps, his robes decorated with images of conquered territories. The emperor doesn't just wake up–he stands up so quickly that he bumps his head on a low-hanging sign that reads "Balkan Powder Keg."

The sign doesn't just hang there–it's literally a powder keg, a massive barrel filled with explosives and decorated with the flags of various Balkan nations. The emperor's collision with the sign causes the keg to tip over, spilling its contents across the street. The powder doesn't just spill–it forms a trail that leads directly to the final cause: the assassination of Archduke Franz Ferdinand, represented by a figure in an old-fashioned car who strikes a match at exactly the wrong moment.

The entire chain becomes a story of cause and effect, with each historical factor leading naturally to the next through vivid, impossible imagery. The student doesn't just memorize the causes–they experience them as part of a coherent narrative that makes the outbreak of war seem inevitable rather than random.

The Professional Detective

The professional folder contains case studies from Detective 369's work with business professionals who need to memorize complex information quickly and accurately. One case involves a sales manager who needed to remember the key features of a new product line–features that were abstract, technical, and difficult to visualize.

The product was a software platform with five key features: scalability, integration, analytics, security, and user-friendliness. Traditional memorization techniques had failed because the terms were too abstract and technical. But Detective 369 helped the manager create a story that transformed these concepts into concrete, memorable images.

The story begins with "Scalability," which becomes "Scale-ability"–a massive balance scale that has the magical ability to grow larger or smaller depending on what's placed on it. The scale is operated by a giant who can adjust its size with the touch of a button, making it perfect for weighing anything from pebbles to planets.

The scale doesn't just sit there–it's connected to a complex machine that represents "Integration." The machine is a massive clockwork device with gears, pulleys, and conveyor belts that connect everything in the office. When the scale measures something, the machine automatically adjusts all the other equipment to match, creating perfect harmony between all the systems.

The machine produces a continuous stream of data that flows like a river toward the next element: "Analytics." This becomes "Anna-lick-tics"–a brilliant female scientist named Anna who has the strange habit of licking computer screens to analyze data. Anna's tongue is so sensitive that she can taste patterns in information, and her licking creates colorful charts and graphs that appear magically on every surface.

Anna's analysis reveals security flaws, which triggers the next element: "Security." This becomes a massive vault with walls made of impenetrable steel, guarded by robots that look like medieval knights. The vault doesn't just protect–it actively hunts down threats, with the robot guards patrolling the area and eliminating any suspicious activity.

The final element is "User-friendliness," which becomes "User-friend-liness"–a magical quality that makes the entire system behave like a friendly, helpful person. The scale smiles and offers encouragement, the integration machine hums pleasant songs while it works, Anna the analyst tells jokes while she licks the screens, and the security robots speak in polite, butler-like voices while they patrol.

The entire product line becomes a story of interconnected characters and magical devices, each one leading naturally to the next through impossible but logical connections. The sales manager doesn't just memorize features–they experience a complete narrative that makes the product's capabilities seem natural and inevitable.

The Lifelong Learner Detective

The third folder contains Detective 369's most challenging cases: helping lifelong learners master foreign languages, where both linking and substitution must work together to overcome the dual barriers of unfamiliar sounds and unfamiliar meanings.

One case involves a learner studying Spanish who was struggling with basic vocabulary. Traditional flashcards and repetition had failed because the Spanish words seemed completely disconnected from their English meanings. But Detective 369 helped create a system where each Spanish word became part of an ongoing detective story.

The word "estar" (to be, for temporary states) becomes "a star"–literally a massive, glowing star that appears in the sky above the learner's house. But this isn't just any star–it's a temporary star that appears only when something important is happening. When the learner needs to remember "estar," they picture this star shining brightly but ready to disappear at any moment, representing the temporary nature of the states it describes.

The star doesn't just shine–it illuminates the next word: "casa" (house), which becomes "case-a"–a massive briefcase that serves as a house. The briefcase is so large that people can live inside it, with rooms and furniture all made from leather and metal clasps. The temporary star shines down on the briefcase-house, creating a connection between location (estar) and place (casa).

The briefcase-house doesn't just sit there–it opens to reveal "perro" (dog), which becomes "pair-o"–a pair of dogs that are so perfectly matched they seem like mirror images of each other. The dogs don't just sit in the briefcase-house–they run out barking, chasing after the next word: "comer" (to eat), which becomes "come-here"–a giant mouth that calls to the dogs, inviting them to come and eat.

Each Spanish word becomes part of an ongoing narrative where Detective 369 investigates the lives and activities of a community of characters. The connections between words aren't just phonetic–they're logical, emotional, and visual. The learner doesn't just memorize translations–they experience Spanish as a living language with its own internal logic and narrative flow.

The Field Assignment: Your Chain of Evidence

Detective 369 closes the three folders and returns to his desk, where he's prepared a special assignment for those ready to join the ranks of memory detectives. This isn't just practice–it's a real case that will test your ability to create mental chains strong enough to hold up under pressure.

Your mission, should you choose to accept it, is to memorize the following 12-item witness statement using only the Linking Method and Substitute Word Method. The statement describes the sequence of events in a complex case, and every detail must be remembered in perfect order.

1. **Telescope**

2. **Electricity**

3. **Photograph**

4. **Helicopter**

5. **Foundation**

6. **Microscope**

7. **Temperature**

8. **Explosion**

9. **Ambulance**

10. **Fingerprint**

11. **Telephone**

12. **Conclusion**

Your task is to create a single, connected narrative where each item leads naturally to the next through bizarre, vivid, and emotionally engaging imagery. Use the Four Rules of Mental Evidence: make things disproportionate, exaggerate numbers, employ violent action, and use substitution when needed.

For the abstract items, use the Substitute Word Method to transform them into concrete, memorable images. "Electricity" might become "Electric-city"—a city where all the buildings are made of lightning bolts. "Temperature" might become "Temper-ature"—an angry creature that gets hot when it's upset.

Your Steps

1. Transform each item into a vivid, specific image, using substitution if necessary.

2. Connect each image to the next through impossible but logical action.

3. Apply the Four Rules to make each connection memorable.

4. Practice the complete chain until you can recall all 12 items in order without looking.

5. Test your memory by having someone else verify your recall.

The goal isn't just to memorize a list–it's to create a mental movie so compelling that your brain will play it automatically whenever you need to recall the information. You should be able to start with "telescope" and let the narrative pull you naturally through all 12 items in perfect sequence.

Remember: the more ridiculous your story, the more memorable it will be. Don't worry about logic or realism–worry about creating connections so strong that forgetting becomes impossible. Your brain will reward creativity with perfect recall.

The Investigation Continues

Detective 369 stands and adjusts his fedora, the chain of evidence now complete and ready for field testing. The Linking Method and Substitute Word

Method aren't just techniques–they're the foundation of all advanced memory work. Master these two approaches, and you'll have the tools to transform any information into unforgettable mental movies.

These methods work because they harness the brain's natural preferences for visual information, narrative structure, and emotional engagement. They transform the abstract into the concrete, the forgettable into the unforgettable, the chaotic into the organized. Most importantly, they turn memorization from a chore into an art form.

As Detective 369 prepares to leave his office, he turns back one final time with a knowing smile. "Every great detective," he says, "knows that the strength of a chain lies not in its individual links, but in the connections between them. You've learned to forge those connections. Now it's time to build your own chains of evidence."

The fog rolls in from the harbor as Detective 369 disappears into the night, but his voice echoes back through the darkness: "The next case is waiting. The Memory Palace door is about to open. And you, detective, are ready to step inside."

Chapter 5: Method of Loci (Memory Palace)

Detective 369 stands before the imposing oak doors of his memory headquarters, brass nameplate gleaming under the flickering streetlight. The building stretches impossibly high into the fog-shrouded night, its countless windows glowing with the warm light of stored knowledge. This isn't just any building–this is his Memory Palace, the most sophisticated evidence storage facility ever constructed. Tonight, he's about to reveal the architectural secrets that have made master detectives legendary for over two thousand years.

The keys jingle softly in Detective 369's weathered hands as he unlocks the main entrance. The Method of Loci, he explains as the heavy doors swing open with a satisfying creak, is the crown jewel of memory techniques. Where other methods create chains of evidence or substitute familiar images for unfamiliar concepts, the Memory Palace creates something far more powerful: a permanent headquarters where any information can be stored, organized, and retrieved with architectural precision.

This technique doesn't just help you remember–it transforms you into the architect of your own mental landscape. Every room becomes a filing cabinet, every piece of furniture becomes a storage device, every corner becomes a hiding place for crucial evidence. The result is a memory system so robust, so expandable, and so reliable that it has been used by everyone from ancient Greek orators to modern-day memory champions.

Detective 369 steps across the threshold, his footsteps echoing in the grand marble foyer. The Method of Loci isn't just a technique–it's a way of thinking, a systematic approach to mental organization that turns the chaos of random information into the ordered architecture of permanent knowledge. Tonight, he's going to teach you how to build your own headquarters, room by room, floor by floor, until you have a mental mansion capable of storing anything you need to remember.

The Ancient Case Files: A Technique Born from Necessity

Detective 369 leads you through the foyer to his first exhibit: a glass case containing ancient scrolls and weathered stone tablets. The Method of Loci, he explains, wasn't invented by memory experts or academic researchers. It was born from practical necessity in the courts and assemblies of ancient Greece, where orators needed to deliver hours-long speeches without notes, where a single forgotten point could mean the difference between victory and defeat.

The technique gets its name from the Latin word "loci," meaning "places," but Detective 369 prefers to think of it as the "Method of Locations." The ancient Greeks discovered that the human brain has an extraordinary capacity for remembering spatial information. You can navigate your childhood home in perfect darkness, remember the exact layout of your first apartment, or find your way through a familiar building even after years of absence. The Memory Palace harnesses this natural spatial intelligence, transforming abstract information into concrete locations that your brain can map and navigate with surprising accuracy.

The legendary story, according to Detective 369's research, involves a Greek poet named Simonides who attended a banquet that ended in tragedy. The roof of the banquet hall collapsed, crushing the guests beyond recognition. But Simonides could identify each victim based on where they had been sitting, because he remembered the exact spatial layout of the room. This terrible event revealed a profound truth: the human mind is naturally equipped to remember spatial relationships with extraordinary precision.

From this insight, ancient orators developed a systematic approach to speech preparation. They would mentally walk through familiar buildings–their homes, temples, or marketplaces–and place each point of their speech at specific locations along the route. During the actual speech, they would mentally retrace their steps, visiting each location in sequence to retrieve the information they had stored there. The result was flawless delivery that seemed almost supernatural to audiences who didn't understand the technique.

Detective 369 has studied the historical records, and the results were remarkable. Orators could deliver speeches lasting several hours without forgetting a single point. They could recall complex legal arguments, detailed historical narratives, and intricate philosophical discussions with perfect accuracy. The technique was so effective that it became the foundation of classical rhetoric education, taught in schools throughout the ancient world.

But the Method of Loci wasn't limited to public speaking. Medieval scholars used it to memorize entire books, creating vast mental libraries that could be accessed instantly. Renaissance thinkers employed it to organize complex philosophical systems, building intellectual palaces that housed centuries of accumulated wisdom. The technique survived wars, plagues, and the fall of empires because it addressed a fundamental human need: the ability to store and retrieve large amounts of information reliably.

Detective 369 closes the glass case and turns to face you directly. What makes this technique so powerful, he explains, is that it works with your brain's natural architecture rather than against it. Your spatial memory system evolved over millions of years to help you navigate complex environments, remember the locations of resources, and find your way back to safety. The Memory Palace simply repurposes this ancient system for modern information storage.

The Blueprint: Understanding Spatial Memory Architecture

Detective 369 leads you up a grand staircase to the second floor, where the walls are covered with architectural drawings, floor plans, and three-dimensional models. This is where he keeps his research on spatial memory-the neurological foundation that makes the Memory Palace possible. Understanding how your brain processes spatial information, he explains, is crucial for building effective memory headquarters.

The hippocampus, that seahorse-shaped structure deep in your temporal lobe, serves as your brain's master architect. It contains specialized cells called "place cells" that fire when you're in specific locations, creating a neural GPS system that maps your environment with remarkable precision. These cells don't just respond to physical locations-they can also encode imaginary spaces, which is why you can mentally navigate buildings that exist only in your mind.

Research by neuroscientists O'Keefe & Nadel has shown that spatial memory operates on multiple scales simultaneously. Grid cells provide the coordinate system, like the latitude and longitude lines on a map. Border cells detect the boundaries of spaces, defining where rooms begin and end. Head direction cells track your orientation, ensuring you know which way you're facing at any given moment. Together, these systems create a comprehensive mental map that can store and retrieve spatial information with extraordinary accuracy.

Detective 369 points to a detailed brain scan displayed on the wall. The key insight, he explains, is that spatial memory and episodic memory are closely linked. When you remember an event, you're not just recalling what happened–you're also remembering where it happened. This is why returning to a childhood neighborhood can trigger floods of memories, why walking through your old school can bring back forgotten experiences, and why certain locations feel charged with emotional significance.

The Memory Palace leverages this natural connection between space and memory. By deliberately placing information in specific locations, you're creating artificial episodes that your brain treats as real experiences. When you mentally walk through your palace, you're not just retrieving abstract data–you're remembering where you put that data, activating the same neural circuits that help you navigate the physical world.

This spatial encoding is remarkably durable. While other forms of memory might fade over time, spatial memories can persist for decades with surprising clarity. Detective 369 can still navigate his childhood home perfectly, even though he hasn't lived there for forty years. This persistence makes the Memory Palace an ideal storage system for information that needs to be retained long-term.

The technique also scales beautifully. You can create simple palaces with just a few rooms for short-term projects, or vast mental complexes with hundreds of locations for comprehensive knowledge systems. The same principles apply regardless of scale: clear pathways, distinct locations, and systematic organization.

The Foundation: Choosing Your Headquarters Location

Detective 369 leads you to the building's cornerstone, a massive granite block inscribed with the words "Location, Location, Location." The first step in building an effective Memory Palace, he explains, is choosing the right foundation. Not all locations are created equal, and the success of your entire system depends on selecting buildings that your brain can navigate effortlessly.

The ideal Memory Palace location should be intimately familiar to you. Detective 369 recommends starting with places where you've spent significant time–your current home, your childhood residence, your workplace, or a school you attended. These locations are already encoded in your long-term memory with rich detail and emotional associations. You can mentally walk through them without conscious effort, which frees up your cognitive resources for storing and retrieving information.

The location should also have a clear, logical pathway. Detective 369 always chooses routes that feel natural and inevitable following the flow of normal movement through the space. In a house, this might mean entering through the front door, moving through the living room, into the kitchen, down the hallway, and into the bedrooms. In an office building, it might mean starting at the elevator, moving through the reception area, past various offices, and ending at the conference room.

Size matters, but not in the way you might expect. Detective 369 has found that medium-sized locations work better than very large or very small ones. A massive shopping mall might seem like it offers more storage space, but it can become confusing and difficult to navigate mentally. A single room might be easy to remember, but it limits your storage capacity. The sweet spot is typically a location with 10-20 distinct storage points–enough to accommodate substantial information without becoming overwhelming.

The emotional tone of the location is also important. Detective 369 prefers places with positive or neutral associations. A childhood home filled with happy memories will feel welcoming and easy to revisit. A stressful workplace might create mental resistance that interferes with effective storage and retrieval. The goal is to create a mental environment where you feel comfortable spending time and where information can be stored without emotional interference.

Distinctiveness is crucial for effective organization. Each location in your Memory Palace should be clearly different from the others, with unique visual characteristics that make them easy to distinguish. Detective 369 looks for locations with varied room sizes, different furniture arrangements, distinct color schemes, and varied lighting conditions. This variety prevents confusion and makes it easier to navigate between different storage areas.

The location should also be stable over time. Detective 369 avoids places that change frequently or that you might forget if you don't visit them regularly. A hotel room you stayed in once might seem vivid now, but it's likely to fade from memory without regular reinforcement. Your home or workplace, on the other hand, are constantly being refreshed in your memory through daily use.

The Construction Phase: Building Your First Memory Palace

Detective 369 opens a thick construction manual and spreads the blueprints across a drafting table. Building your first Memory Palace, he explains, is like constructing any complex structure–it requires careful planning, systematic execution, and attention to detail. But unlike physical construction, this project takes place entirely in your mind, using tools of visualization and association rather than concrete and steel.

The first step is conducting a thorough site survey. Detective 369 recommends starting with a location you know intimately–perhaps your current home. Close your eyes and mentally walk through the space, noting every detail with the precision of a crime scene investigator. Start at the front door and move through the space systematically, room by room, creating a mental inventory of every significant object, piece of furniture, and architectural feature.

Pay special attention to the pathway you follow. Detective 369 emphasizes that consistency is crucial–you should always move through your Memory Palace in the same direction, following the same route every time. This creates a mental highway that becomes more efficient with practice. If you start at the front door and move clockwise through the house, always follow that same pattern. Any deviation can cause confusion and make retrieval more difficult.

As you conduct your survey, identify specific storage locations where you'll place information. Detective 369 recommends choosing objects that are substantial, stable, and visually distinct. A large couch makes a better storage location than a small lamp. A refrigerator is more memorable than a coffee mug. A fireplace is more distinctive than a plain bookshelf. Aim for 10-20 storage locations in your first palace–enough to accommodate substantial information without becoming overwhelming.

Each storage location should be numbered or labeled in a way that makes the sequence clear. Detective 369 uses a simple numbering system: location 1 at the front door, location 2 in the entryway, location 3 in the living room, and so on. This numerical organization provides a backbone for your memory system, ensuring that you can access information in the correct order even if you're tired or distracted.

Once you've identified your storage locations, the next step is practice navigation. Detective 369 recommends spending several days simply walking through your Memory Palace mentally, visiting each location in sequence until the route becomes automatic. You should be able to move from location 1 to location 20 without conscious effort, the way you can walk from your bedroom to your kitchen in the dark.

The key to effective navigation is creating vivid sensory experiences. Don't just visualize the locations–experience them fully. Notice the texture of the doorknob as you enter, the sound of your footsteps on different floor surfaces, the temperature differences between rooms, the quality of light from various windows. The more senses you engage, the more vivid and memorable your palace becomes.

Detective 369 also emphasizes the importance of establishing clear boundaries between locations. Each storage area should feel distinct and separate from the others. If location 5 is the kitchen table, make sure it's clearly different from location 6, which might be the refrigerator. Use physical distance, visual landmarks, or changes in lighting to create clear divisions between storage areas.

The Storage System: Placing Information in Your Palace

Detective 369 leads you to the evidence storage room, where information is transformed into physical objects and carefully placed at specific locations. This is where the abstract becomes concrete, where facts become fixtures, and where your Memory Palace transforms from empty architecture into a fully functional information storage system.

The key to effective storage is creating vivid, impossible associations between abstract information and physical locations. Detective 369 demonstrates this with a simple example: storing the first ten elements of the periodic table. Rather than trying to memorize abstract chemical symbols, he transforms each element into a concrete, memorable object and places it at a specific location in his palace.

At location 1, the front door, Detective 369 places Hydrogen. But this isn't just the word "hydrogen"–it's a giant balloon filled with hydrogen gas, so large that it blocks the entire doorway. The balloon is transparent, allowing you to see the molecular structure swirling inside like a captured storm. When you approach the front door, you can't miss this enormous, floating obstacle that represents the first element.

At location 2, the entryway table, he places Helium. This becomes a party scene where hundreds of helium balloons have been released, their high-pitched voices creating a cacophony of squeaky sounds that echo through the space. The balloons are all different colors, bobbing and floating in impossible profusion, making the entryway feel like a carnival celebration.

Lithium, at location 3, transforms into a massive battery standing in the living room. But this isn't an ordinary battery–it's the size of a refrigerator, crackling with electrical energy and covered in warning labels about lithium content. Sparks fly from its terminals, and the air around it shimmers with heat, creating a dramatic centerpiece that's impossible to ignore.

Each element gets its own distinctive treatment, with the placement logic connecting to the chemical properties when possible. Beryllium becomes a collection of beautiful beryl gems scattered across the coffee table, their green surfaces catching the light like frozen fire. Boron transforms into a bowl of borax that bubbles and steams mysteriously on the kitchen counter. Carbon becomes a pile of coal that has somehow caught fire in the fireplace, burning with unusual intensity.

Detective 369 emphasizes that the key to effective storage is making each item dramatically disproportionate to its surroundings. Everything should be either impossibly large or impossibly small, colored in unnatural hues, or behaving in physically impossible ways. The more outrageous the image, the more memorable it becomes.

The placement process should also engage multiple senses. When Detective 369 places Nitrogen at location 7, he doesn't just visualize liquid nitrogen–he experiences the extreme cold, the white vapor clouds, the sharp hissing sound as it evaporates. The multisensory experience creates a richer memory trace that's easier to retrieve later.

Motion and interaction are crucial elements of effective storage. Static images fade over time, but dynamic scenes remain vivid. Detective 369 makes sure that every item in his Memory Palace is doing something–burning, exploding, moving, transforming, or interacting with other objects. This creates mental movies rather than mental photographs, and movies are far more memorable than still images.

The storage system should also create logical connections between items when possible. Detective 369 often links adjacent locations through cause-and-effect relationships, where the item at location 8 is somehow created or affected by the item at location 7. This creates a narrative flow that makes the entire sequence easier to remember and harder to forget.

The Student Detective: Academic Applications

Detective 369 opens a file marked "Student Cases" and reveals how the Memory Palace transforms academic learning from a chore into an art form. For students, this technique isn't just about memorization–it's about creating organized mental libraries that can accommodate vast amounts of information while making retrieval fast and reliable.

Consider the case of Sarah, a history student struggling to memorize the causes and effects of the American Civil War. Traditional study methods–flashcards, repeated reading, and highlighting–had failed to create lasting memories. But Detective 369 helped her construct a Memory Palace that transformed abstract historical concepts into a vivid, unforgettable narrative.

Sarah's palace was her family's two-story home, a space she knew intimately from childhood. The journey began at the front door, where she encountered the first major cause of the Civil War: slavery. But this wasn't just a word or concept–it was a massive chain made of rusted iron, so heavy that it blocked the entire doorway. The chain was covered in red stains that looked like dried blood, and it rattled ominously whenever the wind touched it. The emotional impact was immediate and unforgettable.

Moving into the living room, Sarah encountered the second cause: economic differences between North and South. This became a dramatic scene where her childhood couch was split perfectly in half–one side covered in industrial machinery representing Northern manufacturing, the other side piled high with cotton bales representing Southern agriculture. The two halves were pulling apart, creating a visible tear in the fabric that grew wider with each passing moment.

The kitchen table held the third cause: states' rights versus federal authority. This transformed into a massive balance scale where one side held a small state capitol building while the other side held an enormous federal building that dwarfed its counterpart. The scale was tipping dangerously toward the federal side, causing documents labeled "states' rights" to scatter across the floor like fallen leaves.

Each cause was connected to its effects through impossible but logical action. The chain at the front door didn't just block entry–it exploded with tremendous force, sending iron links flying throughout the house. These links crashed into the split couch, causing the division to widen further. The unbalanced scale tipped over completely, sending the state capitol tumbling into the dining room where it transformed into the next effect.

The dining room housed the formation of the Confederate States of America, visualized as a dinner party where eleven chairs were arranged around the table, each one occupied by a figure in Confederate gray. But these weren't ordinary dinner guests–they were life-sized chess pieces, moving and speaking in unison as they declared their independence from the federal government.

Sarah's Memory Palace continued through the entire house, with each room containing multiple causes and effects connected through dramatic, impossible imagery. The upstairs bedrooms held the major battles–Gettysburg became a massive cemetery in her childhood bedroom, complete with thousands of tiny tombstones and the ghostly sound of cannon fire. The bathroom transformed into a field hospital where the effects of the war on civilian populations were represented by dramatic scenes of medical care and suffering.

The technique worked because it connected abstract historical concepts to concrete, emotional experiences. Sarah didn't just know that slavery was a cause of the Civil War–she experienced the weight of those chains, felt the emotional impact of the bloodstains, heard the ominous rattling that preceded the explosion. The information wasn't just stored–it was lived.

Detective 369 emphasizes that the student Memory Palace should be organized thematically rather than chronologically when possible. Instead of trying to memorize dates in sequence, focus on creating logical connections between concepts. The causes of the Civil War naturally led to the formation of the Confederacy, which naturally led to the major battles, which naturally led to the war's consequences. This thematic organization makes the information easier to understand and remember.

The Professional Detective: Business Applications

Detective 369 opens another file, this one marked "Corporate Cases," and reveals how business professionals use Memory Palaces to master complex information that directly impacts their careers. In the modern workplace, the ability to remember key facts, figures, and procedures without constant reference to notes can mean the difference between success and mediocrity.

Consider the case of Marcus, a marketing director preparing for a crucial presentation about quarterly sales performance. The presentation involved twelve different product lines, each with multiple metrics including revenue, profit margins, market share, and growth projections. Traditional preparation methods had left Marcus feeling overwhelmed and uncertain about the details that could make or break his presentation.

Detective 369 helped Marcus construct a Memory Palace using his office building–a space where he spent forty hours per week and knew with architectural precision. The journey began at the elevator, where Marcus encountered the first product line: premium headphones. But these weren't ordinary headphones–they were massive, golden devices that filled the elevator shaft, their surfaces covered with dollar signs representing the $2.3 million in quarterly revenue.

The headphones weren't just sitting there–they were playing music so loud that it shook the entire building, with sound waves visible in the air like golden ribbons. The intensity of the music represented the 15% profit margin, with fifteen distinct musical notes floating around the headphones like a visual symphony. The market share (8%) was represented by eight golden speakers positioned around the elevator shaft, each one contributing to the overwhelming auditory experience.

Moving into the reception area, Marcus encountered the second product line: wireless earbuds. These transformed into thousands of tiny flying devices that swarmed through the air like a cloud of electronic bees. The swarm was worth $1.8 million, represented by eighteen massive honeycomb structures that had materialized throughout the reception area. Each honeycomb was dripping with golden honey, representing the 12% profit margin that made this product line particularly sweet.

The conference room held the third product line: gaming headsets. But this wasn't just a meeting space–it had been transformed into a virtual reality gaming arena where twelve massive gaming headsets were engaged in an electronic battle. The headsets were firing laser beams at each other, with each beam worth $100,000 (representing the $1.2 million quarterly revenue). The battle was so intense that it was literally melting the conference table, representing the 18% profit margin that made this product line particularly hot.

Each product line was connected to the next through logical progression and dramatic action. The golden headphones in the elevator created sound waves that attracted the swarm of earbuds in the reception area. The earbuds, in turn, were drawn to the gaming battle in the conference room, where they joined the electronic warfare. This narrative flow made the entire sequence easier to remember and more engaging to experience.

Detective 369 emphasizes that professional Memory Palaces should focus on the information that matters most for decision-making and communication. Revenue figures, profit margins, market share, and growth projections aren't just numbers–they're the foundation of strategic thinking and effective leadership. By storing this information in a Memory Palace, Marcus could access it instantly during presentations, discussions, and strategic planning sessions.

The technique also allows for dynamic updating. When new quarterly figures become available, Marcus can simply update the images in his existing palace rather than learning entirely new information. The $2.3 million golden headphones might become $2.5 million platinum headphones, maintain the same location and basic imagery while reflecting the new reality.

The Lifelong Learner Detective: Personal Knowledge Systems

Detective 369 opens the final file in his collection, labeled "Lifelong Learning Cases," which contains some of his most personally meaningful investigations. These are the cases where individuals use Memory Palaces not for academic requirements or professional obligations, but for the pure joy of learning and the satisfaction of mental mastery.

Consider the case of Elena, a retired teacher who had always wanted to learn Italian but found traditional language learning methods frustrating and ineffective. Vocabulary lists felt abstract and disconnected, grammar rules seemed arbitrary and difficult to remember, and the sheer volume of information felt overwhelming. But Detective 369 helped her construct a Memory Palace that transformed Italian language learning into an immersive cultural experience.

Elena's palace was her dream vacation: a walking tour through Rome that she had planned for years but never taken. The journey began at the Colosseum, where she encountered her first Italian vocabulary theme: family relationships. But instead of abstract words on flashcards, she created a dramatic scene where gladiators representing different family members were engaged in combat.

"Padre" (father) became a massive gladiator with a flowing black beard, his armor decorated with paternal symbols like protective shields and guiding spears. He wasn't just standing there–he was actively fighting to protect "figlia" (daughter), a smaller but fierce gladiator whose armor sparkled with jewels and whose movements were quick and graceful. The battle was so intense that it created visible sparks, representing the emotional bond between father and daughter.

"Madre" (mother) appeared as a gladiator with golden armor that seemed to glow with inner light, her weapons transformed into nurturing tools that somehow remained deadly effective. She was fighting alongside "figlio" (son), whose armor was designed to mirror hers but with masculine touches like broader shoulders and deeper colors. The family was united against a common enemy, creating a memorable scene of cooperation and protection.

Moving to the Pantheon, Elena encountered her second vocabulary theme: food and dining. The ancient temple had been transformed into a massive restaurant where Roman gods were enjoying an Italian feast. "Pane" (bread) became a mountain of golden loaves that reached toward the dome, each one still steaming from divine ovens. The bread was so aromatic that it filled the entire Pantheon with the scent of fresh baking.

"Vino" (wine) transformed into rivers of red and white wine that flowed from the walls like fountains, filling golden chalices that materialized in the hands of every god present. The wine wasn't just flowing–it was singing, with each stream creating musical notes that harmonized with the sounds of divine laughter and conversation.

"Formaggio" (cheese) became a massive wheel of Parmesan that had been placed at the center of the temple, so large that the gods were using it as a table. The cheese was aged to perfection; its surface covered with intricate patterns that told stories of Italian culinary tradition. When the gods cut pieces for their feast, each slice revealed inner layers of different textures and colors.

Elena's Roman journey continued through twelve different locations, each one focused on a specific vocabulary theme and each one connected to the next through logical progression and cultural context. The Spanish Steps became a fashion show where clothing vocabulary was demonstrated by models wearing traditional Italian garments that moved and transformed impossibly. The Trevi Fountain became a transportation hub where different vehicles represented by Italian vocabulary words were racing through the water in a spectacular aquatic rally.

Detective 369 emphasizes that lifelong learning Memory Palaces should be personally meaningful and emotionally engaging. Elena's Italian palace worked because it connected language learning to her personal dreams and cultural interests. The vocabulary wasn't just words–it was part of a story that she wanted to live, a journey that she wanted to take, an experience that she wanted to have.

The technique also allows for natural expansion. As Elena's Italian vocabulary grew, she could add new rooms to her Roman palace or create entirely new palaces in other Italian cities. Florence could house art and culture vocabulary, Venice could contain maritime and travel terms, and the Italian countryside could hold agricultural and nature vocabulary. Each new palace would build on the foundation of spatial memory while creating fresh contexts for new learning.

The Advanced Architecture: Multi-Story Memory Mansions

Detective 369 leads you to a spiral staircase that seems to climb impossibly high into the darkness above. Advanced practitioners of the Memory Palace technique, he explains, don't limit themselves to single-story structures. They create vast mental complexes with multiple buildings, interconnected floors, and specialized storage areas that can accommodate virtually unlimited information.

The key to multi-story construction is maintaining clear organizational principles while expanding capacity. Detective 369 demonstrates this with his own advanced system: a mental skyscraper where each floor is dedicated to a different subject area. The first-floor houses current case files, the second floor contains forensic procedures, the third floor holds legal knowledge, and so on. Each floor follows the same navigational principles as a simple Memory Palace, but the building as a whole creates a comprehensive knowledge management system.

Vertical navigation between floors requires special attention to transition points. Detective 369 uses elevators, staircases, and even fantastical devices like teleportation chambers to move between different knowledge domains. Each transition point is marked by distinctive imagery that signals the shift from one subject area to another. The elevator that takes him from current cases to forensic procedures is decorated with crime scene tape and evidence markers, creating a clear psychological boundary between different types of information.

The advanced architecture also allows for cross-referencing between different knowledge areas. Detective 369 can create connections between floors through windows, balconies, or even impossible architectural features like bridges that span between buildings. When a current case requires specific forensic knowledge, he can literally look up from his first-floor case file to see the relevant information stored three floors above.

Multi-building complexes represent the ultimate expression of Memory Palace architecture. Detective 369 has created an entire mental city where different buildings house different aspects of his professional and personal knowledge. The police station holds his detective work, the university contains his academic interests, the library houses his reading notes, and his home stores personal memories and family information. Each building follows its own internal logic while contributing to the overall knowledge ecosystem.

The key to managing complex Memory Palace systems is maintaining regular maintenance and review. Detective 369 schedules weekly walks through his various palaces, updating information, reinforcing storage locations, and ensuring that the architectural integrity remains intact. Just as physical buildings require upkeep, mental palaces need regular attention to prevent decay and maintain optimal functionality.

Advanced practitioners also develop specialized storage techniques for different types of information. Numbers might be stored using specific visualization methods, names might be connected to biographical details, and procedures might be encoded as step-by-step journeys through dedicated palace sections. Each type of information gets its own optimized storage approach while fitting into the overall architectural framework.

The Field Assignment: Constructing Your Personal Headquarters

Detective 369 returns to his desk and opens a thick construction manual labeled "Your Assignment." This isn't just practice–it's the foundation of your personal memory empire, the beginning of a system that can grow and evolve with your needs for years to come.

Your mission is to construct your first Memory Palace and use it to store the following information: the twelve cranial nerves of the human nervous system. This is a classic memory challenge that requires precise recall, making it a perfect test for your new headquarters.

For this exercise, focus on memorizing the names in the correct order:

1. **Olfactory**
2. **Optic**
3. **Oculomotor**
4. **Trochlear**
5. **Trigeminal**
6. **Abducens**
7. **Facial**
8. **Vestibulocochlear**
9. **Glossopharyngeal**
10. **Vagus**
11. **Accessory**
12. **Hypoglossal**

Your Steps

1. **Select Your Palace:** Choose a location you know intimately, like your current home.
2. **Define Your Route:** Mentally walk through the space and identify 12 distinct storage locations (loci) along a logical path.
3. **Create Your Images:** Transform each cranial nerve into a vivid, memorable image using the Substitute Word Method (e.g., "Olfactory" becomes a giant, sniffing nose; "Optic" becomes a glowing eyeball).
4. **Place Your Images:** Place each image at its designated location with dramatic, impossible, and engaging action.

5. **Practice and Recall:** Walk through your palace mentally until the route and the images are automatic. Test your recall by listing all twelve nerves in order. Once you've mastered the basic sequence, experiment with adding additional information to each location. What does each cranial nerve control? Where is it located in the brain? What happens if it's damaged? Your Memory Palace can accommodate layers of information, turning a simple list into a comprehensive knowledge system.

Remember that construction is an iterative process. Your first palace might feel awkward or unstable, but this is normal. Detective 369's first Memory Palace was a modest affair with only five storage locations. Through practice and refinement, it grew into the vast mental complex you've explored tonight. Start small, focus on mastering the fundamentals, and let your system evolve naturally as your skills develop.

The Master Detective's Revelation: Why Memory Palaces Transform Minds

Detective 369 stands at the window of his penthouse office, looking out over the vast cityscape of interconnected Memory Palaces that stretch to the horizon. The Method of Loci, he reflects, isn't just a memory technique–it's a fundamental shift in how you relate to information and knowledge. It transforms you from a passive recipient of facts into an active architect of understanding.

The technique works because it leverages your brain's most sophisticated and durable memory systems. Spatial memory evolved over millions of years to help humans navigate complex environments and remember the locations of crucial resources. When you build a Memory Palace, you're not fighting against your brain's natural tendencies–you're harnessing them for intellectual purposes.

But the benefits extend far beyond simple memorization. Detective 369 has discovered that Memory Palace practitioners develop enhanced visualization skills, improved spatial reasoning, and stronger associative thinking. The act of creating vivid mental imagery strengthens your imagination and creativity. The practice of navigating complex mental structures enhances your ability to understand and manipulate abstract concepts.

The technique also creates a unique form of mental discipline. Building and maintaining Memory Palaces requires consistent practice, systematic organization, and attention to detail. These skills transfer to other areas of life, improving your ability to manage complex projects, organize information effectively, and think systematically about challenging problems.

Perhaps most importantly, Memory Palaces give you ownership of your knowledge. Information stored in external systems–books, computers, or databases–remains external. But information stored in your Memory Palace becomes part of your mental furniture, available instantly whenever you need it. This creates a foundation of confidence and competence that transforms how you approach learning and problem-solving.

Detective 369 has seen this transformation in countless students, professionals, and lifelong learners. They don't just become better at memorizing–they become better at thinking, learning, and understanding. The Memory Palace technique doesn't just store information–it transforms minds.

The Investigation Continues: Building Your Mental Empire

Detective 369 turns from the window and walks toward the door, his investigation complete but his work far from finished. The Memory Palace technique, he explains, is both a destination and a journey. You can use it immediately to solve specific memory challenges, but its true power emerges over time as you build larger and more sophisticated systems.

Your first palace will be modest–perhaps a single room or a small apartment. But as your skills develop, you'll find yourself creating vast mental complexes with specialized areas for different types of information. The technique scales beautifully, growing with your needs and ambitions.

The key to long-term success is consistency and patience. Detective 369 has been building and refining his Memory Palace system for decades, and he's still discovering new applications and improvements. Start with simple projects, master the fundamentals, and let your system evolve organically as your understanding deepens.

Remember that the Memory Palace is ultimately a tool for freedom. Freedom from the anxiety of forgetting important information, freedom from dependence on external memory aids, and freedom to engage with complex ideas without being overwhelmed by their details. It's a tool that serves you rather than controlling you, a system that enhances your natural abilities rather than replacing them.

Detective 369 pauses at the threshold, his hand on the brass doorknob. The fog outside has begun to lift, revealing the clear outline of the city below. Similarly, the fog of confusion that surrounds memory work begins to clear when you understand the principles and practice the techniques. The Memory Palace method isn't just about memorization–it's about mastery.

The detective tips his fedora and steps into the morning light. Your mental headquarters awaits construction, your first palace is ready to be built, and the techniques for architectural excellence are now in your hands. The investigation into advanced memory techniques continues, but you're no longer just an observer–you're a participant, an architect, a master of your own mental domain.

Chapter 6: Active Recall and Spaced Repetition

Detective 369 sits in his dimly lit interrogation room, a single lamp casting harsh shadows across the metal table. Across from him sits a suspect–but this isn't an ordinary criminal. This suspect is far more elusive, more dangerous: a fading memory. The detective knows that passive questioning won't work here. He can't simply read the case file over and over, hoping the truth will emerge. No, this requires the Interrogation Method–a technique so powerful it can force even the most stubborn memories to confess their secrets.

In the world of memory investigation, Detective 369 has learned that there are two fundamental truths that separate the amateurs from the professionals. First, you must interrogate your memories actively rather than passively reviewing evidence. Second, you must know exactly when to revisit a cold case—not too soon, not too late, but at the **precise** moment when the memory is about to slip away forever.

These aren't just techniques–they're the core principles that transform ordinary minds into extraordinary ones. Active Recall, what Detective 369 calls the Interrogation Method, forces your brain to work for information rather than spoon-feeding it easy answers. Spaced Repetition, his Cold Case Protocol, ensures that important information never truly goes cold, always returning to your consciousness just when you need it most.

Tonight, Detective 369 reveals the secrets of these two powerful methods, showing you how to become a master interrogator of your own mind and a skilled manager of your mental case files. The techniques you're about to learn aren't just memory tricks–they're the foundation of all serious learning, backed by over a century of scientific research and proven effective in countless real-world investigations.

The Interrogation Method: Active Recall Revealed

Detective 369 adjusts the lamp, creating a pool of bright light in the center of the table. The Interrogation Method, he explains, is based on a simple but profound principle: the act of retrieving information from memory makes that information stronger, more accessible, and more durable. It's not enough to simply expose yourself to facts repeatedly–you must actively wrestle with them, force them to emerge from the depths of your consciousness, and prove that they truly belong in your long-term memory.

Most people, Detective 369 has observed, study the way they investigate crimes–passively. They read reports, review evidence, and flip through photographs, hoping that repeated exposure will somehow make the information stick. But Detective 369 knows better. The real breakthroughs come not from staring at evidence, but from asking the right questions, testing theories, and forcing the mind to work actively rather than simply absorb passively.

The science behind the Interrogation Method is as compelling as it is robust. Research by cognitive psychologists like Roediger & Karpicke has consistently shown that retrieval practice–the formal term for what Detective 369 calls active recall–produces significantly better learning outcomes than passive review. When you force your brain to retrieve information from memory, you're not just testing what you know–you're strengthening the neural pathways that store that information, making it easier to access in the future.

The power of this method lies in what researchers call the "testing effect" or "retrieval practice effect." Each time you successfully recall information from memory, you're essentially rewiring your brain, strengthening the connections between neurons and creating more robust memory traces. It's like Detective 369's interrogation techniques–the more you practice questioning suspects, the better you become at extracting the truth. The more you practice retrieving memories, the stronger those memories become.

But there's another crucial element that makes the Interrogation Method so effective: the struggle is the point. When Detective 369 questions a difficult suspect, he doesn't expect immediate answers. The resistance, the effort required to break through barriers–that's what makes the eventual confession so much more valuable. Memory works the same way. The more effort required to retrieve information, the stronger the memory becomes once it's successfully accessed.

Detective 369 demonstrates this principle with a simple experiment. He shows you a list of facts about a complex case–witness statements, timelines, evidence locations. Then he gives you two choices: you can either reread the list five times, or you can read it once and then spend the remaining time trying to recall as much as possible without looking. Most people choose the first option because it feels easier and more comfortable. But Detective 369 knows that the second option–the Interrogation Method–will produce dramatically better results.

The reason is neurological. When you simply reread information, you're using what psychologists call "recognition memory"–the ability to identify information when it's presented to you. But when you actively recall information, you're engaging "retrieval memory"–the ability to generate information from scratch. Recognition might help you identify a suspect in a lineup, but retrieval allows you to describe that suspect from memory when no lineup is available. In the real world, retrieval is far more valuable than recognition.

The Cold Case Protocol: Spaced Repetition Mastery

Detective 369 walks to a wall covered with case files, each one marked with specific dates and review schedules. This is his Cold Case Protocol–the systematic approach to ensuring that important information never truly goes cold. The secret, he explains, isn't just knowing when to interrogate your memories, but knowing when to revisit them for optimal retention.

The foundation of this protocol lies in understanding the enemy that every memory detective faces: the forgetting curve. First documented by Hermann Ebbinghaus in 1885, this phenomenon shows that human memory follows a predictable pattern of decay. Within 24 hours of learning something new, most people forget approximately 50-80% of the information. The loss is rapid at first, then gradually levels off, creating the characteristic curve that has haunted students and professionals for over a century.

But Detective 369 has discovered that this curve isn't inevitable–it's defeatable. The key lies in understanding that each time you successfully retrieve information from memory, you reset the forgetting curve. The information doesn't just return to its original strength–it becomes stronger than before, taking longer to fade the next time. This is the principle that makes spaced repetition so powerful: by reviewing information at strategically timed intervals, you can transform fragile memories into permanent knowledge.

The timing of these reviews is crucial. Detective 369 has learned that there's an optimal window for revisiting each piece of information–not too soon, when the memory is still fresh and the review provides little benefit, and not too late, when the memory has faded so much that you're essentially relearning rather than reinforcing. The sweet spot is just before the memory is about to disappear, when the retrieval requires effort but is still possible.

Research has shown that this optimal timing follows a predictable pattern. The first review should occur within 24 hours of initial learning. The second review should happen after 2-3 days. The third review should be scheduled for about a week later. Subsequent reviews can be spaced at increasingly longer intervals–two weeks, one month, three months, and so on. Each successful retrieval pushes the next review further into the future, gradually building memories that can last a lifetime.

Detective 369 has refined this basic schedule through years of practical application. He's learned that the intervals must be adjusted based on the difficulty of the material, the importance of the information, and the individual's learning patterns. Easy facts might need only three or four spaced reviews to become permanent, while complex concepts might require a dozen or more strategic encounters over several months.

The Cold Case Protocol also accounts for failure. When Detective 369 can't retrieve information during a scheduled review, he doesn't abandon the case–he adjusts the timeline. Failed retrievals are moved back to shorter intervals, as if the case has become active again and requires more frequent attention. This adaptive approach ensures that no important information is ever truly lost, while allowing well-learned material to fade gracefully into the background.

The Science of Memory Interrogation

Detective 369 opens a thick research file labeled "Neurological Evidence" and spreads the contents across the table. The Interrogation Method and Cold Case Protocol aren't just intuitive techniques–they're based on decades of rigorous scientific research that reveals exactly how memory works at the cellular level.

When you engage in active recall, you're triggering a complex cascade of neurological events that strengthen memory traces throughout your brain. The process begins in the hippocampus, that seahorse-shaped structure deep in your temporal lobe that serves as the brain's memory consolidation center. Each time you successfully retrieve information, you're reactivating the same neural networks that were involved in the original learning, causing those networks to fire in sync and strengthen their connections.

This strengthening occurs through a process called long-term potentiation (LTP), where synaptic connections between neurons become more efficient and durable. The more often specific neural pathways are activated through retrieval practice, the stronger and more permanent those pathways become. It's like Detective 369's interrogation techniques–the more often you use a particular line of questioning, the more automatic and effective it becomes.

The research also reveals why spaced repetition is so much more effective than massed practice (cramming). When you review information at spaced intervals, you're forcing your brain to reconstruct the memory from scratch each time, rather than simply maintaining it in active working memory. This reconstruction process requires more effort and engages more neural systems, creating more robust and transferable memories.

Cognitive load theory provides another layer of explanation for why these methods work. When you're actively recalling information, you're not just retrieving isolated facts–you're rebuilding the entire context in which those facts were learned. This comprehensive reconstruction creates what psychologists call "elaborative encoding," where each piece of information becomes connected to multiple other pieces, creating a web of associations that makes the entire network more stable and accessible.

The forgetting curve itself has been validated and refined through modern neuroscience. Brain imaging studies show that newly formed memories undergo a gradual process of systems consolidation, where they're transferred from temporary storage in the hippocampus to more permanent storage in the neocortex. This process takes time–often months or even years–and it's during this vulnerable period that memories are most susceptible to forgetting. Spaced repetition works by repeatedly reactivating these consolidating memories, ensuring that they successfully make the transition to permanent storage.

The Student Detective: Academic Applications

Detective 369 pulls out a case file marked "Academic Investigations" and reveals how students can transform their learning through strategic interrogation and cold case management. The traditional approach to studying–reading textbooks, highlighting notes, and reviewing flashcards–is like trying to solve crimes by staring at evidence without asking any questions. The Interrogation Method and Cold Case Protocol turn passive students into active investigators of their own knowledge.

Consider Sarah, a pre-med student struggling with the vast amount of information required for her anatomy and physiology courses. Traditional study methods had left her feeling overwhelmed and uncertain about her mastery of the material. But Detective 369 taught her to approach her studies like a skilled interrogator, using active recall to test her knowledge and spaced repetition to ensure long-term retention.

Sarah's transformation began with the Interrogation Method. Instead of simply rereading her textbook chapters, she learned to create questions about the material and then test herself rigorously. When studying the cardiovascular system, she didn't just review diagrams of the heart–she covered the labels and forced herself to identify each structure from memory. She didn't just read about cardiac cycles–she drew the pressure and volume curves from scratch, testing her understanding of how the heart works.

The key insight that Detective 369 taught Sarah was that difficulty during study is not a sign of failure–it's a sign of learning. When she struggled to remember the names of heart valves or the sequence of electrical conduction, she wasn't failing–she was strengthening the neural pathways that would eventually make this information automatic. The effort required to retrieve information was building the memories she needed for long-term success.

Sarah's Cold Case Protocol was equally systematic. She organized her review schedule using a digital spaced repetition system that tracked when each piece of information needed to be revisited. Facts about basic anatomy that she mastered quickly were scheduled for review at longer intervals, while complex physiological processes that gave her trouble were brought back for more frequent interrogation. The system ensured that nothing important was ever forgotten, while allowing her to focus her time and energy on the material that needed the most attention.

The results were dramatic. Sarah's exam scores improved significantly, but more importantly, her confidence and understanding deepened. She was no longer just memorizing facts for tests–she was building a comprehensive knowledge base that would serve her throughout her medical career. The information she learned using these methods didn't disappear after exams–it became part of her permanent intellectual toolkit.

Detective 369 emphasizes that the student application of these methods requires discipline and initial effort. The Interrogation Method feels harder than passive review because it is harder–your brain is working to build stronger memories. The Cold Case Protocol requires organization and consistency because effective spaced repetition depends on precise timing. But students who master these techniques find that they spend less time studying while achieving better results, because they're working with their brain's natural learning mechanisms rather than against them.

The Professional Detective: Workplace Applications

Detective 369 opens another case file, this one marked "Professional Investigations," and reveals how working professionals can use these methods to master the complex information that drives career success. In the modern workplace, the ability to learn quickly, retain important information, and apply knowledge effectively often determines who advances and who gets left behind.

Consider Marcus, a financial analyst who needed to master a complex new regulatory framework that was reshaping his industry. The traditional approach–reading through hundreds of pages of documentation, attending training sessions, and hoping the information would stick–had left him feeling unprepared and anxious about implementing the new requirements. Detective 369 taught him to treat this professional learning challenge like a complex investigation requiring systematic interrogation and strategic case management.

Marcus's transformation began with applying the Interrogation Method to his professional learning. Instead of simply reading regulatory documents, he learned to create scenarios and test his understanding. When studying new compliance requirements, he didn't just read about the rules–he created hypothetical situations and forced himself to determine how the regulations would apply. He didn't just review procedural changes–he walked through complex transactions step by step, testing his ability to identify potential compliance issues.

The key insight that Detective 369 shared with Marcus was that professional knowledge isn't just about knowing facts–it's about being able to apply those facts quickly and accurately under pressure. Active recall doesn't just help you remember information–it helps you practice the mental processes you'll need to use that information effectively in real-world situations. When Marcus forced himself to recall regulatory requirements from memory, he wasn't just strengthening his memory–he was rehearsing the analytical skills he would need in his daily work.

Marcus's Cold Case Protocol was adapted to the realities of professional life. He used a combination of digital tools and physical reminders to ensure that important information was reviewed at optimal intervals. New regulations that he was still learning were scheduled for frequent review, while well-established procedures were checked less often but never forgotten entirely. The system ensured that his knowledge stayed current and accessible, even as new information was constantly being added to his professional toolkit.

The professional applications of these methods extend far beyond individual learning. Detective 369 has worked with entire teams to implement systematic approaches to knowledge management and skill development. Sales teams use active recall to master product knowledge and practice handling objections. Medical professionals use spaced repetition to maintain their knowledge of procedures and drug interactions. Legal teams use these methods to stay current with evolving case law and regulatory changes.

The results in professional settings are often dramatic. Employees who master these techniques find that they can learn new skills more quickly, retain important information more reliably, and apply their knowledge more effectively under pressure. They become more confident in their expertise and more valuable to their organizations. Most importantly, they develop a systematic approach to continuous learning that serves them throughout their careers.

The Lifelong Learner Detective: Personal Knowledge Systems

Detective 369 opens his final case file, marked "Personal Investigations," which contains some of his most satisfying cases–instances where individuals have used these methods not for academic or professional requirements, but for the pure joy of learning and intellectual growth. These are the cases that remind him why he became a memory detective in the first place: the transformative power of systematic learning applied to personal passions and interests.

Consider Elena, a retired teacher who had always dreamed of learning Italian but found traditional language learning methods frustrating and ineffective. Vocabulary seemed to disappear as quickly as she learned it, grammar rules felt arbitrary and disconnected, and the sheer volume of information felt overwhelming. Detective 369 helped her transform her approach to language learning by treating it like a complex investigation requiring systematic interrogation and strategic case management.

Elena's transformation began with applying the Interrogation Method to vocabulary acquisition. Instead of simply reading word lists or using traditional flashcards, she learned to create rich contexts for new words and then test her ability to recall them in various situations. When learning the Italian word "casa" (house), she didn't just memorize the translation–she created mental scenarios where she needed to use the word, tested her ability to recall it in different contexts, and practiced incorporating it into complete sentences.

The key insight that Detective 369 shared with Elena was that language learning isn't just about memorizing words–it's about building the mental flexibility to use those words fluently and naturally. Active recall doesn't just help you remember vocabulary–it helps you practice the mental processes you'll need to use that vocabulary in real conversations. When Elena forced herself to recall Italian words from memory, she wasn't just strengthening her memory–she was rehearsing the cognitive skills she would need for actual communication.

Elena's Cold Case Protocol was carefully designed to match the natural rhythm of language acquisition. New vocabulary was scheduled for frequent review, while well-established words were checked less often but never forgotten entirely. Grammar concepts that she found difficult were brought back for regular interrogation, while rules that came naturally were allowed to fade into the background. The system ensured that her Italian knowledge grew steadily and systematically, building on a foundation of truly mastered material.

The personal applications of these methods extend far beyond language learning. Detective 369 has worked with individuals pursuing everything from musical instrument mastery to historical research, from cooking skills to art appreciation. The principles remain the same: active interrogation builds stronger memories than passive review, and strategic spacing ensures that important information remains accessible over time.

What makes personal learning applications so rewarding is the intrinsic motivation that drives them. When people use these methods to pursue their genuine interests and passions, they discover that learning becomes not just more effective, but more enjoyable. The challenge of active recall becomes a game, the systematic approach of spaced repetition becomes a satisfying routine, and the gradual accumulation of knowledge becomes a source of deep personal satisfaction.

The Advanced Interrogation Techniques

Detective 369 walks to a locked cabinet and withdraws a folder marked "Advanced Methods." These are the sophisticated techniques that separate expert memory detectives from novices–the methods that can be applied when basic active recall and spaced repetition need to be enhanced for particularly challenging information or complex learning goals.

1. Layered Interrogation: Instead of simply asking yourself to recall information, you create multiple levels of questioning that test different aspects of your knowledge. For factual information, you might ask: "What is this?" "Why is this important?" "How does this connect to what I already know?" "What examples can I generate?" "What would happen if this were different?" Each layer of questioning forces you to engage with the material in a different way, creating multiple retrieval pathways and deeper understanding.

2. Predictive Recall: Instead of just testing your memory of what you've already learned, you force yourself to predict what you might learn next, or to anticipate how current information might be applied in new situations. This technique transforms passive knowledge into active expertise by forcing you to think like the experts in your field, anticipating patterns and connections that go beyond mere memorization.

3. Cross-Domain Interrogation: Detective 369 has found that the most robust memories are created when you can connect information across different domains of knowledge. Instead of learning isolated facts within narrow categories, you systematically look for connections between what you're learning and what you already know in other areas. This creates a web of associations that makes information more meaningful and more durable.

4. Failure Analysis: When you can't recall information during an interrogation session, instead of simply looking up the answer, you analyze why the retrieval failed. Was the original encoding insufficient? Are there interfering memories? Is the retrieval cue inadequate? This analytical approach turns failed recalls into learning opportunities, helping you strengthen weak points in your memory system.

These advanced techniques require more time and effort than basic active recall, but they produce correspondingly deeper and more durable learning. Detective 369 uses them for the most important information in his professional and personal knowledge base–the core concepts and skills that he needs to access quickly and accurately under any circumstances.

The Anki Application: Your Digital Memory Partner Detective 369 straightens a stack of index cards on his desk, but these aren't the dog-eared cards of old–they're digital, dynamic, and smarter than anything the city's ever seen. Enter Anki, the open-source application that brings active recall and spaced repetition into the twenty-first century.

Anki–meaning "memorization" in Japanese–is more than just a flashcard app. It's a detective's digital partner, designed to make facts, names, dates, and details unforgettable. Each time you review a card, Anki's algorithm calculates when you're likely to forget, then schedules it for review at just the right moment. That's spaced repetition in action, and it's how the world's top students, medics, and memory athletes train their minds.

Setting up is easy. Download Anki for free at apps.ankiweb.net. The software works on Windows, Mac, Linux, iPhone, and Android, syncing your decks across devices like a master case file always at hand.

New to Anki? The best starting point is the Anki Manual, with step-by-step instructions and video guides. For detective-grade tactics, online forums and YouTube channels offer deep dives on card formatting, tagging, and custom study routines.

But here's where the case gets interesting: today, you don't have to build every card by hand. Artificial Intelligence–like the detective's own informant network–can help you generate flashcards, summarize textbooks, or even create custom decks on any topic in seconds. AI tools can scrape key facts from articles, organize material into question-and-answer format, and suggest optimal learning schedules–leaving you more time for investigation, less time for paperwork.

Every detective needs the right tools. With Anki and AI in your arsenal, your memory work just got a whole lot smarter.

The Field Assignment: Your Personal Investigation

Detective 369 closes the advanced methods folder and turns his attention to you. This isn't just theory–it's a practical system that you can begin implementing immediately. Your mission, should you choose to accept it, is to conduct a systematic investigation of your own learning using both the Interrogation Method and the Cold Case Protocol.

Your assignment has two phases, each designed to test different aspects of these techniques. The first phase will test your mastery of active recall by challenging you to learn and retain a specific set of information using only interrogation methods. The second phase will test your ability to implement spaced repetition by creating and following a systematic review schedule over several weeks.

Phase One: The Interrogation Challenge

Select a topic that's important to your current goals–this could be professional knowledge, academic material, or personal interest. The topic should be substantial enough to require genuine effort (not something you could memorize in a single session) but focused enough to be manageable (not an entire textbook or course). Good examples might include: the key concepts in a specific chapter of a professional development book, the vocabulary for a particular theme in a foreign language you're learning, or the biographical details of 20 historical figures in a field that interests you.

Your task is to learn this information using only the Interrogation Method. This means no passive reading, no highlighting, no traditional note-taking. Instead, you'll create questions about the material and then test yourself relentlessly. Start by scanning the material quickly to get a general sense of what's covered. Then, instead of reading carefully, create questions that you think the material should answer. Finally, use the material to answer your questions, but force yourself to recall the answers from memory rather than simply reading them.

Track your progress by keeping a simple log of what you can and cannot recall during each interrogation session. Don't worry about perfect performance– the struggle is the point. Each failed retrieval is actually strengthening your memory for the next attempt. Continue this process until you can answer all of your questions from memory with confidence.

Phase Two: The Cold Case Protocol

Once you've mastered the material from Phase One, your task is to implement a systematic spaced repetition schedule to ensure long-term retention. Create a simple tracking system (this could be a spreadsheet, a notebook, or a digital app) that records when each piece of information needs to be reviewed next.

Start with the basic schedule that Detective 369 has taught you: first review after 24 hours, second review after 2-3 days, third review after one week, and subsequent reviews at increasingly longer intervals. But adapt this schedule based on your performance. Information that you recall easily can be scheduled for longer intervals, while information that gives you trouble should be brought back for more frequent review.

Continue this process for at least four weeks, tracking both your recall accuracy and your confidence level for each piece of information. Pay special attention to how the difficulty of recall changes over time–you should find that information becomes easier to remember with each successful retrieval, allowing you to space the reviews further apart.

Success Metrics

Detective 369 has established specific criteria for determining whether you've successfully mastered these techniques. For the Interrogation Method, success means being able to recall the target information from memory without prompts or cues, under conditions that are more challenging than those in which you learned it. For the Cold Case Protocol, success means maintaining high recall accuracy while gradually extending the intervals between reviews.

But the real measure of success is more profound: your entire approach to learning will be transformed. Information that once seemed impossible to remember will now feel manageable. The anxiety that often accompanies complex learning will be replaced by confidence in your systematic approach. Most importantly, you will discover that these methods don't just help you remember more—they empower you to understand more deeply and think more clearly about whatever you're learning.

The Master Detective's Revelation

Detective 369 stands and walks to the window, looking out at the city lights that sparkle in the darkness like neural connections in the vast network of human knowledge. The Interrogation Method and Cold Case Protocol, he reflects, aren't just memory techniques–they're fundamental approaches to learning that can transform how you relate to information and knowledge throughout your life.

The research is clear and compelling: active recall produces significantly better learning outcomes than passive review, and spaced repetition creates memories that can last a lifetime. But the scientific evidence only tells part of the story. The real power of these methods lies in how they change your relationship with learning itself. When you become skilled at interrogating your own knowledge, you develop a confidence and competence that extends far beyond any specific subject matter.

Detective 369 has seen this transformation in countless students, professionals, and lifelong learners. They don't just become better at memorizing–they become better at thinking, problem-solving, and applying knowledge in novel situations. The discipline required to implement these methods consistently develops mental habits that serve them in all areas of life. The systematic approach to knowledge management becomes a foundation for continuous growth and development.

Perhaps most importantly, these methods create a sense of ownership over your own learning. When you actively interrogate your knowledge and systematically manage your memory, you're not just consuming information–you're creating understanding. The knowledge you develop through these methods doesn't feel borrowed or temporary–it feels like a natural extension of your own thinking.

The techniques also scale beautifully with your ambitions. You can use them to master a single chapter for an upcoming exam, or to build comprehensive expertise in a professional field over many years. The principles remain constant while the applications expand to match your goals and interests. This scalability makes them valuable not just for immediate learning challenges, but for the lifelong pursuit of knowledge and growth.

The Investigation Continues

Detective 369 turns from the window and walks toward the door, his investigation complete but his work far from finished. The Interrogation Method and Cold Case Protocol are tools that will serve you throughout your life, growing more powerful and more natural with practice. They're not just techniques to be learned–they're skills to be developed, refined, and personalized to match your unique learning style and goals.

The key to long-term success with these methods is consistency and patience. Detective 369 has been refining his approach to active recall and spaced repetition for decades, and he's still discovering new applications and improvements. Start with simple implementations, master the basic principles, and let your system evolve organically as your understanding deepens.

Remember that these techniques work best when they're integrated into a comprehensive approach to learning. The Interrogation Method becomes more powerful when combined with the visualization techniques from earlier chapters. The Cold Case Protocol becomes more efficient when organized within the Memory Palace framework. These methods don't replace the other techniques in your toolkit–they enhance them, creating a synergistic system that's more powerful than any individual component.

Most importantly, remember that the goal isn't just to remember more information–it's to think more clearly, learn more efficiently, and develop the intellectual confidence that comes from true mastery. The Interrogation Method and Cold Case Protocol are means to this end, tools that help you become not just a better memorizer, but a better thinker and learner.

Detective 369 pauses at the threshold, his hand on the brass doorknob. The fog outside has begun to lift, revealing the clear outline of the city below. Similarly, the fog of confusion that surrounds effective learning begins to clear when you understand and apply these proven methods. Active recall and spaced repetition aren't just memory techniques–they're the foundation of all serious learning.

The detective tips his fedora and steps into the morning light. Your interrogation skills are sharp, your cold case protocol is established, and the systematic approach to memory mastery is now in your hands. The investigation into advanced memory techniques continues, but you're no longer just an observer–you're a participant, an interrogator, a master of your own mental evidence.

Chapter 7: The Alphabet PEG System

Detective 369 stands before a massive filing cabinet that stretches from floor to ceiling, its brass nameplate gleaming under the harsh fluorescent light of the evidence room. Twenty-six drawers line the cabinet in perfect order, each one labeled with a single letter of the alphabet. This isn't just any filing system—this is the A-Z Evidence Archive, the most elegant organizational tool in the detective's arsenal. Tonight, he's about to reveal how this alphabetical framework can transform any list, any collection of facts, into a perfectly organized mental filing system that never loses track of crucial information.

In the shadowy world of criminal investigation, Detective 369 has learned that organization can make the difference between a solved case and a cold file. Evidence scattered randomly across a desk becomes useless clutter, but evidence filed systematically becomes a weapon of precision. The Alphabet PEG System operates on this same principle, transforming the twenty-six letters of the alphabet into a comprehensive filing cabinet that lives entirely in your mind.

This technique represents one of the most intuitive and immediately useful tools in the memory detective's toolkit. Where other systems require complex calculations or elaborate spatial constructions, the Alphabet PEG System builds upon knowledge you've possessed since childhood. Every letter from A to Z becomes a concrete image, a mental file folder capable of holding any information you need to organize and retrieve.

Detective 369 has used this system to organize witness statements, categorize evidence types, and maintain comprehensive case files that span decades of investigation. The beauty of the system lies in its perfect balance of structure and flexibility–organized enough to prevent chaos, flexible enough to accommodate any type of information that crosses your path.

The Filing Cabinet: Understanding Alphabetical Architecture

Detective 369 walks slowly along the length of the filing cabinet, his fingers trailing across each drawer's brass label. The Alphabet PEG System, he explains, transforms the natural order of the alphabet into a sophisticated storage mechanism where each letter corresponds to a specific, memorable image. These images become the pegs–the hooks upon which you hang whatever information needs to be filed and retrieved.

The foundation of this system lies in creating a permanent, unchanging image for each letter of the alphabet. Unlike other memory techniques that might use different images for different purposes, the Alphabet PEG System demands consistency. Once you've chosen your image for the letter A, it remains your A-image forever. This consistency creates a reliable framework that becomes more powerful and automatic with each use.

Detective 369 demonstrates this principle by opening the first drawer of his cabinet. The letter A corresponds to "Apple"–not just any apple, but a specific, vivid image of a bright red apple with a single green leaf, gleaming as if it had just been polished. This apple appears in Detective 369's mind instantly whenever he encounters the letter A, creating an immediate visual anchor for whatever information needs to be filed in the first position.

The selection of images for each letter follows principles that Detective 369 has refined through decades of practical application. The best alphabet images are concrete nouns that create immediate, vivid mental pictures. Abstract concepts like "ambition" or "analysis" might seem intellectually appropriate for the letter A, but they lack the visual impact necessary for effective memory work. The apple works because it's concrete, colorful, and instantly recognizable.

Each image should also be emotionally neutral and personally meaningful. Detective 369 chose "apple" not because it's the most common A-word, but because it creates a pleasant, stable image that he can use repeatedly without emotional interference. The goal isn't to be clever or creative with each letter–it's to build a reliable, unchanging framework that serves you consistently over time.

The images should also be distinctly different from each other to prevent confusion. Detective 369 carefully avoided selecting images that might be similar in size, color, or category. His B-image is "Balloon," creating a visual contrast with the apple–where the apple is solid and earthy, the balloon is light and airy. This deliberate differentiation ensures that each letter occupies its own distinct mental space.

Detective 369 emphasizes that the process of selecting your alphabet images is one of the most important investments you'll make in your memory system. These images will serve you for years, appearing in countless memory tasks and becoming as automatic as the alphabet itself. Take the time to choose images that resonate with you personally, that create vivid mental pictures, and that feel comfortable to use repeatedly.

The Evidence Archive: Building Your Personal A-Z System

Detective 369 pulls out a thick leather-bound notebook and opens it to reveal hand-drawn sketches of twenty-six distinct objects, each one labeled with its corresponding letter. This is his personal alphabet archive–the collection of images that has served him faithfully through thousands of cases and decades of investigation.

The process of building your personal A-Z system begins with systematic selection, moving through the alphabet letter by letter and choosing images that will serve you reliably over time. Detective 369 walks through his complete system, explaining the logic behind each choice and the qualities that make certain images more effective than others.

A is for **Apple,** chosen for its vivid color, simple shape, and universal recognition. Detective 369 visualizes this apple as perfectly red, sitting on a wooden table in a pool of warm sunlight. The image is pleasant, stable, and immediately accessible whenever he needs to file information in the first position.

B is for **Balloon,** selected to create contrast with the apple while maintaining visual clarity. Detective 369's balloon is bright blue, floating at eye level, gently swaying in an invisible breeze. The movement adds life to the image while keeping it simple enough to use repeatedly without fatigue.

C is for **Cat,** chosen for its dynamic potential and emotional appeal. Detective 369's cat is a sleek black feline with bright green eyes, sitting alertly with its tail curved around its paws. The cat's ability to move and interact makes it particularly useful for creating memorable associations with filed information.

D is for **Dog,** selected to complement the cat while maintaining distinct characteristics. Detective 369's dog is a golden retriever with a friendly expression, tongue hanging out slightly, radiating warmth and loyalty. The emotional warmth of the dog image makes it particularly effective for filing positive or important information.

E is for **Elephant,** chosen for its impressive size and memorable features. Detective 369's elephant is gray with wise eyes and large ears, standing majestically in an open savanna. The elephant's size and dignity make it perfect for filing important or weighty information.

F is for **Fish**, selected for its graceful movement and aquatic environment. Detective 369's fish is a bright orange goldfish swimming in crystal-clear water, its fins moving rhythmically as it glides through its liquid world. The fluid movement creates a sense of life and energy that enhances memorability.

Detective 369 continues through the entire alphabet, each image chosen for its specific qualities and its relationship to the overall system: **G** is for **Guitar**, **H** for **House**, **I** for **Ice cream**, **J** for **Jar**, **K** for **Kite**, **L** for **Lamp**, **M** for **Moon**, **N** for **Nest**, **O** for **Orange**, **P** for **Pencil**, **Q** for **Queen**, **R** for **Rose**, **S** for **Ship**, **T** for **Tree**, **U** for **Umbrella**, **V** for **Violin**, **W** for **Watch**, **X** for **X-ray**, **Y** for **Yacht**, and **Z** is for **Zebra**.

Each image in Detective 369's system has been tested through years of practical use, refined through countless applications, and proven effective across diverse information types. The guitar resonates with musical energy, the house provides shelter and security, the ice cream brings sweetness and pleasure. Every image carries its own emotional signature while maintaining the consistency necessary for systematic organization.

The key to building an effective personal system lies in understanding that these images will become deeply integrated into your thinking patterns. Detective 369 can no longer think of the letter M without seeing his moon, can't encounter the letter S without visualizing his ship. This automatic association is what makes the system so powerful–the alphabet becomes a collection of vivid mental objects rather than abstract symbols.

The Filing Protocol: Organizing Information Alphabetically

Detective 369 walks to his desk and picks up a case file marked "Witness Statements–Robbery Investigation." Inside are twenty-three separate statements from different witnesses, each one containing crucial information that must be organized and remembered systematically. This is where the Alphabet PEG System reveals its true power–transforming chaotic information into ordered knowledge.

The filing protocol begins with the fundamental principle of the peg system: each alphabet image serves as a hook for hanging information. Detective 369 doesn't just memorize lists–he creates associations between list items and his alphabet images, building memorable connections that make retrieval automatic and reliable.

To demonstrate this process, Detective 369 takes the first witness statement and associates it with his A-image. The witness described seeing a suspicious man in a red jacket. Rather than simply trying to remember "red jacket," Detective 369 creates a vivid scene where his bright red apple is wearing a tiny red jacket, the fabric stretched comically around the fruit's curved surface. The absurdity of the image makes it memorable, while the connection to the apple ensures that it will be filed in the A-position.

The second witness mentioned hearing a car backfire. Detective 369 associates this with his B-image by imagining his blue balloon suddenly popping with a loud bang, the rubber pieces flying in all directions like debris from a backfiring car. The sound and motion create a memorable scene that links the witness information to the B-position in his mental filing system.

The third witness saw the suspect drop something near a tree. Detective 369 connects this to his C-image by visualizing his black cat climbing that tree, its green eyes scanning the ground below for whatever was dropped. The cat's hunting behavior creates a natural association with the act of searching for dropped objects.

Detective 369 emphasizes that the key to effective filing lies in creating bizarre, impossible, emotionally engaging connections between the alphabet images and the information being filed. Logical associations are often forgettable, but absurd connections stick in memory like evidence at a crime scene. The more outrageous the association, the more likely it is to survive the natural forgetting process.

The system also accommodates different types of information through adaptable association techniques. Factual information might be connected to alphabet images through visual similarity, emotional content, or phonetic relationships. Procedural information might be filed by having the alphabet images perform the required actions. Abstract concepts might be connected through metaphorical relationships that make the intangible tangible.

Detective 369 demonstrates this flexibility by filing different types of evidence using the same alphabet framework. Scientific data becomes visual experiments performed by his alphabet images. Historical dates become time periods that his images are transported to. Foreign vocabulary becomes actions or objects that his images interact with. The alphabet provides the consistent structure while the associations adapt to match the information's unique characteristics.

The protocol also includes systematic review procedures that ensure filed information remains accessible over time. Detective 369 regularly walks through his alphabet, visiting each image and rehearsing the associations he's created. This mental filing review prevents information from becoming buried in the archive and ensures that crucial evidence remains available when needed.

The Student Detective: Academic Applications

Detective 369 opens a file labeled "Academic Investigations" and reveals how students can transform their study habits by implementing the A-Z filing system. The traditional approach to academic memorization–lists, flashcards, and repetitive reading–often leaves students feeling overwhelmed by the sheer volume of information. But the Alphabet PEG System provides a structured framework that makes even the most challenging academic material manageable.

Consider Sarah, a biology student struggling to memorize the various systems of the human body. Traditional study methods had left her confused about which organs belonged to which systems and how the different systems interacted. Detective 369 taught her to use the Alphabet PEG System to create a comprehensive filing system for anatomical information.

Sarah's transformation began with organizing the major body systems alphabetically. The circulatory system became associated with her A-image, an apple. But this wasn't just any apple–it was an apple with a visible network of red veins running through its skin, pulsing with blood-like juice. The image was so vivid that Sarah could never forget which system was filed under A.

The digestive system was filed under D, associated with her dog image. Sarah visualized her golden retriever eating enthusiastically, its digestive process visible through a transparent stomach. The dog's obvious pleasure in eating created a memorable connection to the digestive system's function, while the D-position provided perfect alphabetical organization.

The endocrine system found its place under E, connected to Sarah's elephant image. She imagined her elephant's various glands as visible lumps under its gray skin, each one secreting colorful hormones that flowed through the elephant's massive body like paint through water. The elephant's size reflected the endocrine system's body-wide influence, while the E-position kept it properly filed.

Sarah's system continued through the entire alphabet, with each body system receiving its own dedicated filing space. The immune system became associated with her I-image, ice cream, which she visualized as defending itself against bacterial invasion. The muscular system connected to her M-image, the moon, which she imagined flexing and contracting like a giant muscle in the night sky.

Detective 369 emphasizes that Sarah's success came from understanding how to layer detailed information within each alphabetical filing position. The circulatory system file didn't just contain the basic concept–it housed specific organs, functions, and diseases. The apple image became a comprehensive folder where heart information was filed in the apple's core, blood vessel information was stored in the veins on the skin, and circulation disorders were represented by brown spots on the apple's surface.

The system also accommodated the interconnected nature of biological systems. When Sarah needed to remember how the circulatory and respiratory systems worked together, she could visualize her apple (circulatory) and her R-image, a rose (respiratory), exchanging gases through their shared stem. The connection between images reflected the biological connection between systems.

Academic applications of the Alphabet PEG System extend far beyond biology. Detective 369 has worked with history students who file historical periods alphabetically, with each era represented by vivid scenes involving their alphabet images. Literature students organize character analyses, themes, and plot points using the A-Z framework. Language students file vocabulary, grammar rules, and cultural information within their personal alphabet archive.

The key to academic success with this system lies in understanding that education isn't just about memorizing facts–it's about building organized knowledge structures that support understanding and application. The Alphabet PEG System provides this structure, creating a framework where information can be systematically stored, reviewed, and retrieved as needed.

The Professional Detective: Workplace Applications

Detective 369 opens another case file, this one marked "Corporate Investigations," and reveals how business professionals can leverage the A-Z filing system to master the complex information landscapes of modern workplaces. In professional environments, the ability to organize and recall vast amounts of information quickly and accurately often determines career success.

Consider Marcus, a marketing manager who needed to master detailed product information for twenty-six different items in his company's catalog. Traditional approaches–spreadsheets, notes, and repeated review–had left him feeling uncertain about product details during crucial client meetings. Detective 369 taught him to transform his product knowledge into a comprehensive A-Z filing system that made information instantly accessible.

Marcus's transformation began with assigning each product to a specific letter of the alphabet based on systematic criteria. Products were organized alphabetically by their primary function, target market, or distinctive feature. The key was creating a logical assignment system that would remain consistent over time, preventing confusion and making the filing process automatic.

Product A was their flagship accounting software, which Marcus associated with his A-image, an apple. But this wasn't just any apple–it was an apple covered in tiny numbers and mathematical symbols, with a calculator growing out of its stem. The image captured both the alphabetical position and the product's function, creating a memorable filing system that made product details instantly accessible.

Product B was their business intelligence platform, filed under Marcus's B-image, a balloon. He visualized this balloon as transparent, filled with swirling data points and graphs that were visible through its surface. The balloon floated above a cityscape of office buildings, representing how the platform provided an elevated view of business operations.

Product C was their customer relationship management system, associated with Marcus's C-image, a cat. He imagined this cat as extraordinarily social, surrounded by dozens of other cats that it was somehow managing and organizing. The cat wore a tiny headset and carried a digital tablet, representing the system's communication and organization capabilities.

Each product in Marcus's catalog received its own dedicated filing position, with the alphabet images serving as permanent anchors for detailed information. The accounting software file contained pricing structures, feature comparisons, and competitive advantages. The business intelligence file housed technical specifications, implementation timelines, and client success stories. The CRM file contained integration capabilities, training requirements, and support options.

Detective 369 emphasizes that Marcus's success came from understanding how to create rich, multifaceted associations within each alphabetical position. The apple image didn't just represent the accounting software–it became a comprehensive filing cabinet where different aspects of the product were stored in different parts of the apple. Pricing information was filed in the apple's core, technical specifications were stored in the flesh, and competitive advantages were represented by the apple's bright, attractive skin.

The system also accommodated dynamic information that changed regularly. When product prices were updated, Marcus didn't need to relearn everything–he simply updated the relevant section of his existing image. When new features were added, they were incorporated into the existing alphabetical framework rather than creating entirely new memory structures.

Professional applications of the Alphabet PEG System extend across industries and job functions. Sales professionals use it to organize client information, product details, and competitive intelligence. Healthcare workers file patient information, treatment protocols, and medical procedures. Legal professionals organize case precedents, statutory requirements, and procedural guidelines. The system's flexibility allows it to adapt to any professional context while maintaining its essential organizational advantages.

The key to professional success with this system lies in understanding that workplace information isn't just about individual facts–it's about building comprehensive knowledge networks that support decision-making and problem-solving. The Alphabet PEG System provides this network, creating a framework where professional information can be systematically stored, updated, and retrieved as needed.

The Lifelong Learner Detective: Personal Knowledge Systems

Detective 369 opens his final case file, marked "Personal Investigations," which contains some of his most meaningful work–helping individuals organize and master information that enriches their personal lives and intellectual pursuits. These cases remind him why he became a memory detective in the first place: the joy of learning and the satisfaction of organized knowledge.

Consider Elena, a retired teacher who had decided to pursue her lifelong dream of learning about world cultures. The traditional approach–reading travel guides, watching documentaries, and taking notes–had left her feeling overwhelmed by the sheer breadth of cultural information. Detective 369 taught her to create a comprehensive A-Z filing system for organizing her cultural knowledge.

Elena's transformation began with organizing world cultures alphabetically by country, creating a systematic framework for her global studies. Each letter of the alphabet became home to specific countries and their associated cultural information. The A-position housed information about Argentina, Australia, and Austria. The B-position contained details about Brazil, Belgium, and Bangladesh. The systematic organization made it easy to add new cultural information while maintaining clear mental organization.

Elena's A-image, an apple, became her filing cabinet for Argentine culture. She visualized this apple performing a passionate tango, its red skin swirling like a dancer's dress, while the sounds of Spanish guitar emanated from its core. The apple's dance moves incorporated traditional Argentine foods–empanadas appeared as dance partners, while mate tea flowed like liquid music around the dancing fruit.

Her B-image, a balloon, became the repository for Brazilian culture. Elena imagined this balloon as carnival-colored, bouncing rhythmically to samba music while tropical fruits and exotic birds swirled around it. The balloon's surface displayed the colors of the Brazilian flag, while its movement captured the energy and joy of Brazilian celebrations.

Her C-image, a cat, housed Chinese cultural information. Elena visualized this cat as wise and dignified, practicing tai chi movements while surrounded by traditional Chinese symbols. The cat's green eyes reflected the color of jade, its whiskers twitched with ancient wisdom, and its movements demonstrated the graceful balance of Chinese philosophy.

Each cultural file contained multiple layers of information organized within the alphabet image framework. The Argentine apple held information about history in its core, geography in its skin, language in its stem, and cuisine in its flesh. The Brazilian balloon contained historical information in its string, geographical details in its surface, cultural practices in its air, and artistic traditions in its colors.

Detective 369 emphasizes that Elena's success came from understanding how to create personally meaningful connections between the alphabet images and the cultural information she was learning. The images weren't just storage containers–they became living representations of cultural experiences that she wanted to have. The dancing apple made her want to visit Argentina, the carnival balloon inspired dreams of Rio de Janeiro, and the wise cat created interest in Chinese philosophy.

The system also accommodated Elena's evolving interests and expanding knowledge. When she discovered a fascinating aspect of Australian Aboriginal culture, she could easily file it within her A-position alongside her existing Argentine and Austrian information.   When she learned about Belgian chocolate-making traditions, the information found its natural place in her B-position with her Brazilian cultural files.

Personal applications of the Alphabet PEG System extend to countless areas of individual interest and growth. Cooking enthusiasts organize recipes, techniques, and culinary traditions. Art lovers file information about artists, movements, and historical periods. Music fans organize composer biographies, musical styles, and performance details. The system's flexibility allows it to grow with personal interests while maintaining organizational clarity.

The key to personal success with this system lies in understanding that lifelong learning isn't just about accumulating facts–it's about building rich, interconnected knowledge networks that enhance understanding and appreciation. The Alphabet PEG System provides this network, creating a framework where personal interests can be systematically explored, organized, and enjoyed.

The Advanced Filing Techniques: Master-Level Organization

Detective 369 walks to a specialized cabinet marked "Advanced Protocols" and withdraws a folder containing his most sophisticated organizational techniques. These methods represent the pinnacle of A-Z filing mastery, approaches that allow experienced practitioners to handle complex information with extraordinary efficiency and precision.

The first advanced technique is what Detective 369 calls "Nested Filing." Instead of using each alphabet position for a single piece of information, advanced practitioners create sub-filing systems within each letter. The A-position doesn't just hold one item–it becomes a complete filing cabinet with its own internal organization. This exponentially increases the system's capacity while maintaining the simple A-Z structure.

Detective 369 demonstrates this technique using his A-image, the apple. Instead of filing just one piece of information with the apple, he creates a systematic approach where different parts of the apple hold different types of information. The apple's core holds the most important information, the flesh contains supporting details, the skin houses surface-level facts, and the stem connects to related information in other alphabetical positions.

Within the apple's core, Detective 369 can file up to ten additional pieces of information using a numerical sub-system. Core position 1 might hold the most crucial fact, core position 2 contains the second most important detail, and so on. This nested approach allows a single alphabet position to accommodate complex, multi-layered information while maintaining easy retrieval.

The second advanced technique is "Cross-Referencing," where Detective 369 creates systematic connections between different alphabetical positions. Information rarely exists in isolation–facts relate to other facts, concepts connect to other concepts, and understanding emerges from seeing these relationships. Advanced practitioners use their alphabet images to create visible connections that reflect these information relationships.

Detective 369 illustrates this technique by showing how his A-image (apple) might connect to his T-image (tree). When filing information about apple cultivation, he doesn't just store the facts with the apple–he creates a visible connection where the apple is hanging from his tree image. This connection allows him to access related information about orchards, seasonal growing patterns, and agricultural techniques through the tree-apple relationship.

The third advanced technique is "Dynamic Reorganization," where Detective 369 adapts his filing system to accommodate changing information needs. Real-world information doesn't remain static–priorities shift, new facts emerge, and organizational needs evolve. Advanced practitioners develop systematic approaches for updating their A-Z filing systems without losing the investment made in original organization.

Detective 369 has developed protocols for handling these changes that maintain the integrity of his alphabet framework. When information becomes outdated, he doesn't just delete it–he transforms it into historical context that enriches his understanding of current information. When new facts emerge, he integrates them into existing alphabetical positions rather than creating entirely new organizational structures.

The fourth advanced technique is "Contextual Adaptation," where Detective 369 adjusts his alphabet images to match the specific requirements of different information types. The same A-image might appear differently when filing scientific information versus literary analysis versus historical facts. The apple retains its essential character while adapting its appearance to enhance the memorability of specific information types.

These advanced techniques require significant practice and systematic development, but they transform the Alphabet PEG System from a simple organizational tool into a sophisticated information management system capable of handling professional-level complexity while maintaining the accessibility that makes the basic system so effective.

The Field Assignment: Your A-Z Investigation

Detective 369 closes the advanced protocols folder and turns his attention to you. This assignment will test your ability to create and implement a complete Alphabet PEG System, proving that you can transform any collection of information into an organized, accessible mental filing system.

Your mission consists of three phases, each building upon the previous one to create a comprehensive understanding of how the A-Z filing system works in practice. Success at each phase demonstrates mastery of increasingly sophisticated organizational skills.

Phase One: Building Your Personal Archive

Your first challenge is to create your own complete A-Z image system. This requires selecting twenty-six distinct images, one for each letter of the alphabet, that will serve as your permanent filing framework. These images will become as familiar to you as the alphabet itself, appearing automatically whenever you need to file or retrieve information.

Begin by working through the alphabet systematically, selecting images that meet Detective 369's criteria for effective alphabet pegs. Each image should be concrete, vivid, emotionally neutral, and distinctly different from the others. Avoid abstract concepts, similar images, or emotionally charged selections that might interfere with systematic use.

Write down your complete A-Z system and spend several days practicing the sequence until it becomes automatic. You should be able to mentally walk through your alphabet images as easily as reciting the letters themselves. This automatic access is what makes the system practical for real-world applications.

Test your system by having someone else call out random letters while you instantly visualize the corresponding image. The goal is to achieve the same level of **automaticity** that Detective 369 has developed—immediate, effortless access to any alphabet position without conscious effort.

Phase Two: Systematic Filing Practice

Your second challenge involves using your A-Z system to organize and memorize a specific collection of information. Choose a list of twenty-six items that you actually need to remember–this could be a professional task, academic material, or personal interest. The key is selecting real information that has practical value in your life.

Apply your alphabet filing system to this information, creating memorable associations between each list item and its corresponding alphabet image. Follow Detective 369's principles of creating bizarre, impossible, emotionally engaging connections that make the associations unforgettable.

Practice recalling your filed information until you can access any item instantly by thinking of its alphabetical position. Test your system by having someone else call out random letters while you immediately recall the associated information. The goal is to demonstrate that alphabetical organization makes information more accessible, not more difficult to remember.

Phase Three: Advanced Integration

Your final challenge involves combining your A-Z system with other memory techniques you've learned. Create a comprehensive approach that uses alphabetical organization as the foundation while incorporating visualization, association, and spatial memory techniques to enhance effectiveness.

Choose a complex information set that requires sophisticated organization-perhaps a professional knowledge base, academic subject matter, or comprehensive personal interest. Apply your integrated system to organize this information, demonstrating that the Alphabet PEG System becomes more powerful when combined with other memory techniques.

Practice navigating your integrated system until it feels natural and efficient. You should be able to access any information quickly, update the system as information changes, and expand the organizational framework as your knowledge grows. The goal is to create a personalized information management system that serves your specific needs while maintaining the organizational advantages of alphabetical structure.

The Master Detective's Revelation: Why Order Conquers Chaos

Detective 369 stands at his window, looking out at the city streets where thousands of people navigate their daily lives with the help of organized systems-street signs, addresses, directories, and databases. The Alphabet PEG System, he reflects, represents a fundamental principle of human cognition: the power of imposed order to create meaning from chaos.

The effectiveness of alphabetical organization lies in its perfect balance of structure and flexibility. The structure provides a reliable framework that prevents information from becoming lost or confused. The flexibility allows any type of information to be accommodated within the system. This balance makes the A-Z approach simultaneously powerful and accessible, suitable for both simple lists and complex knowledge management.

Detective 369 has discovered that the Alphabet PEG System also enhances understanding, not just memory. When you organize information alphabetically, you're forced to think about relationships, categories, and connections. The act of deciding which information belongs under which letter creates analytical thinking that deepens comprehension. You're not just memorizing facts-you're building organized knowledge structures.

The system also addresses one of the fundamental challenges of information management: the problem of retrieval. Having information isn't useful unless you can access it when needed. The alphabetical framework provides multiple pathways to any piece of information–you can access it through direct alphabetical lookup, through associative connections, or through contextual relationships. This redundancy makes the system remarkably robust and reliable.

Perhaps most importantly, the Alphabet PEG System gives you ownership of your information. Instead of being dependent on external organizational systems, you become the master of your own knowledge. The information doesn't just exist in your mind–it lives there in an organized, accessible form that serves your specific needs and interests.

Detective 369 has seen this transformation in countless students, professionals, and lifelong learners. They don't just become better at organizing information–they become more confident in their ability to handle complex knowledge, more creative in their thinking, and more effective in their decision-making. The A-Z system isn't just a memory technique–it's a foundation for intellectual empowerment.

The Investigation Continues: Building Your Information Empire

Detective 369 turns from the window and walks toward the door, his investigation complete but his work far from finished. The Alphabet PEG System, he explains, is both a destination and a journey. You can use it immediately to organize specific information, but its true power emerges over time as you build comprehensive knowledge systems that serve your evolving needs.

Your first applications will be modest–perhaps a simple list or a basic organizational task. But as your skills develop, you'll find yourself creating sophisticated information architectures where thousands of facts are instantly accessible through alphabetical pathways. The technique scales beautifully, growing with your ambitions and adapting to your changing requirements.

The key to long-term success with the Alphabet PEG System is consistency and systematic development. Detective 369 has been refining his approach for decades, and he's still discovering new applications and improvements. Start with simple implementations, master the basic principles, and let your system evolve organically as your understanding deepens.

Remember that the A-Z system is ultimately a tool for intellectual freedom. Freedom from the chaos of disorganized information, freedom from the anxiety of forgotten facts, and freedom to engage with complex knowledge confidently and systematically. It's a tool that serves you rather than controlling you, a system that enhances your natural abilities rather than replacing them.

Detective 369 pauses at the threshold, his hand on the brass doorknob. The fog outside has begun to lift, revealing the clear outline of the city below. Similarly, the fog of information overload begins to clear when you master the Alphabet PEG System. Random facts become organized knowledge, chaotic information becomes systematic understanding, and overwhelmed minds become organized ones.

The detective tips his fedora and steps into the morning light. Your A-Z filing cabinet is constructed, your alphabetical images are selected, and the techniques for systematic organization are now in your hands. The investigation into advanced memory techniques continues, but you're no longer just an observer–you're a participant, an organizer, a master of alphabetical memory.

The scattered evidence that once threatened to overwhelm now stands ready to be filed, organized, and retrieved with alphabetical precision. Detective 369 has shown you the system, taught you the techniques, and revealed the secrets of organized memory. The case files are labeled, the evidence is sorted, and the investigation continues.

The eighth case file closes with the satisfied snap of a well-organized filing system engaging. Detective 369 has revealed the secrets of the Alphabet PEG System–the technique that transforms chaotic information into organized knowledge, random facts into systematic understanding, and overwhelmed minds into precisely organized ones. The filing cabinet is built, the system is mastered, and the investigation continues toward the numerical precision that awaits in the world of the Major System.

The Alphabet Peg System gave us a powerful way to organize information using the 26 letters of the alphabet. But what happens when the information you need to remember isn't alphabetical at all? Numbers are everywhere—phone numbers, dates, statistics, historical timelines, and more.

Chapter 8: The Major System - From Digits to Words

Detective 369 stands before his evidence board, studying a series of numbers that seem to mock him from their neat rows across the cork surface. Phone numbers, dates, case file numbers, suspect identification codes—all the numerical breadcrumbs that could make or break an investigation. To the untrained eye, these digits are just random sequences, cold and forgettable. But Detective 369 knows better. Hidden within these seemingly meaningless strings lies a pattern, a code that once cracked transforms the most elusive numbers into unforgettable mental images.

Sometimes, numbers are the perfect culprits in the crime of forgetfulness. They're everywhere–lurking in phone contacts, hiding in PINs, masquerading as years and statistics. They slip away the moment your back is turned, leaving you fumbling for your notebook or frantically searching your phone. But Detective 369 has spent decades perfecting the art of numerical investigation, and tonight he's about to reveal his most powerful tool: the Major System, a phonetic decoder ring that transforms cold digits into vivid mental cinema.

The Major System isn't just another memory trick–it's a complete cryptographic solution to the mystery of numerical recall. This technique, with roots stretching back to 17th-century memory masters, represents one of the most elegant and powerful approaches to number memorization ever devised. When you master this system, you don't just remember numbers–you decode them, transforming abstract sequences into concrete images that stick in your memory like evidence in a solved case.

The Cipher: Understanding the Phonetic Code

Detective 369 walks to his desk and opens a worn leather journal, its pages filled with the fruits of decades of investigation. The Major System, he explains, is built on a simple but profound principle: every digit from 0 to 9 corresponds to specific consonant sounds. These sounds become the building blocks of words, and these words become the foundation of unforgettable images.

The beauty of this phonetic approach lies in its logical structure. Each digit-to-sound mapping has been carefully chosen to create natural, memorable associations that make the system easier to learn and harder to forget. Detective

369 demonstrates this principle by revealing the complete numerical cipher that has served him throughout his career.

The Major System: Phonetic Code

Digit	Consonant Sounds	Mnemonic / How to Remember
0	S, Z	The word "zero" begins with the Z sound.
1	T, D	The digit **1** has one downstroke, like a **t**.
2	N	The letter **n** has two downstrokes.
3	M	The letter **m** has three downstrokes.
4	R	The word "four" ends with the R sound.
5	L	The Roman numeral for 50 is **L**.
6	J, SH, CH, soft G	The digit **6** looks like a backwards **J**.
7	K, hard C, hard G	Two **7**s can be arranged to form the letter **K**.
8	F, V	A handwritten **f** looks similar to the digit **8**.
9	P, B	The digit **9** is a mirror image of the letter **P**.

Detective 369 emphasizes that mastering these digit-to-sound relationships is like learning the alphabet of numerical memory. Once these connections become automatic, any number can be quickly converted into memorable words and images. But the real power of the Major System emerges when you understand how to apply these basic mappings to create comprehensive numerical stories.

Breaking the Code: From Sounds to Images

Detective 369 steps back from his journal and approaches a whiteboard covered with numerical examples. The process of converting numbers to images, he explains, requires more than just knowing the digit-to-sound mappings. It demands the ability to think creatively, to see possibilities where others see only cold digits, and to transform abstract sequences into concrete mental movies.

The key principle that Detective 369 has mastered is simple: **vowels have no numerical value.** The letters A, E, I, O, and U serve only as fillers, allowing you to create meaningful words from the consonant sounds. This flexibility is what makes the Major System so powerful—you're not limited to specific words, but can create any word that fits the consonant pattern while being memorable and meaningful to you.

Detective 369 demonstrates this principle with a simple example. The number 32 breaks down into the sounds M (3) and N (2). By adding vowels, this becomes "moon," creating an immediate image of a celestial body glowing in the night sky. But the same number could also become "man," "mine," or "mean," depending on which vowels you choose and which image would be most memorable in context.

The process becomes even more interesting with longer numbers. Detective 369 shows how the number 415 converts to R (4), T or D (1), and L (5). Following the consonant sounds R-T-L, this could become "rattle," creating a vivid image of a rattlesnake coiled and ready to strike. The same number could also become "retail," "rathole," or "riddle," each offering different narrative possibilities.

Detective 369 emphasizes that the goal isn't to find the "correct" word for a number, but to find the word that creates the most memorable image for your specific purpose. A phone number might be best remembered through concrete nouns, while a date might be more memorable when converted to action words. The system's flexibility allows you to adapt your encoding to match your memory's natural preferences.

The process of creating memorable images from these words follows the same principles that Detective 369 has taught throughout his investigation. The images should be vivid, exaggerated, and emotionally engaging. A simple moon becomes a massive lunar disk that fills the entire sky. A rattlesnake becomes a coiled serpent with diamond-pattern scales that catch the light like precious gems. The more outrageous and impossible the image, the more memorable it becomes.

Detective 369 also reveals one of his most important techniques: the use of action and interaction. Static images fade over time, but dynamic scenes remain vivid in memory. When he needs to remember the number 647, he converts it to the sounds J (6), R (4), and K (7), creating the word "jerk." But he doesn't just imagine a person–he creates a scene where this character is performing some dramatic action, perhaps jerking a rope that triggers a cascade of other events.

The Major System also accommodates special cases and variations that make it even more powerful. Detective 369 explains that double letters are counted only once unless they're pronounced separately. The word "ladder" would be L-D-R (541), not L-D-D-R. Silent letters are ignored entirely–"knee" is just N (2), not K-N. And certain letter combinations follow special rules: "X" is treated as K-S (70), "GH" is usually ignored unless pronounced as F or G, and "Z" becomes 10 when pronounced "TS" as in "pizza."

These nuances might seem complex initially, but Detective 369 emphasizes that they become intuitive with practice. The system is designed to follow natural speech patterns, making it feel organic rather than artificial. As you develop fluency with the Major System, you'll find yourself automatically applying these rules without conscious thought.

Case Studies: The System in Action

Detective 369 opens three specific case files from his archives, each one demonstrating how the Major System transforms different types of numerical challenges into manageable memory tasks. These aren't theoretical examples–they're real-world applications that show the system's versatility and power across different contexts and requirements.

The Student Detective: Academic Number Mastery

Detective 369 first shares the case of Maria, a history student who was struggling to memorize the complex chronology of World War II. Traditional date memorization had left her feeling overwhelmed by the sheer volume of years, each one blending into the next in a confusing historical blur. But when Detective 369 taught her the Major System, the dates transformed from abstract numbers into vivid historical scenes.

Maria's breakthrough came when she learned to convert years into memorable images using the Major System. The year 1941, when Germany invaded the Soviet Union, became "tape" (19) and "rat" (41). Rather than simply remembering these words, Maria created a dramatic scene where a massive rat was gnawing through important military tapes, symbolizing how the invasion tore apart the Nazi-Soviet pact. The image was so vivid and emotionally engaging that the date became unforgettable.

The D-Day landing in 1944 became "paper" (19) and "robe" (44), which Maria visualized as military papers wrapped in a ceremonial robe being carried ashore at Normandy. The bombing of Hiroshima in 1945 became "paper" (19) and "roll" (45), creating an image of burning paper rolling through the destroyed city. Each date became part of a larger narrative tapestry where historical events were connected through memorable imagery.

Detective 369 emphasized that Maria's success came from understanding how to layer the Major System with other memory techniques. She placed her date-images within a Memory Palace based on her campus, creating a historical walking tour where each building represented a different year of the war. She used the Linking Method to connect related events, creating narrative chains that showed cause and effect relationships. The result was a comprehensive understanding of World War II chronology that served her throughout her academic career.

Maria's system also incorporated statistical information that had previously seemed impossible to remember. The number of casualties at specific battles, the tonnage of supplies moved during major operations, the distances involved in military campaigns–all became memorable through conversion to vivid imagery. The 6,000 ships involved in D-Day became "shoes" (6) and "sauce" (00), creating a scene where thousands of military boots were marching through a sea of red sauce, symbolizing the scale of the operation and the bloodshed it entailed.

The Professional Detective: Business Intelligence

Detective 369's second case study features Marcus, a financial analyst responsible for presenting complex datasets during high-stakes quarterly meetings.

Relying on spreadsheets left Marcus anxious and disconnected from the numbers. With the help of the Major System, he transformed raw financial data into a fluent mental language–allowing him to speak confidently and accurately without notes.

Marcus's challenge was to memorize key performance indicators across several product lines: revenue figures, profit margins, market shares, and growth projections. Detective 369 showed him how to convert each number into a vivid image using the Major System, making abstract figures concrete and memorable.

The flagship product's quarterly revenue of $2.3 million became "name" (2 = n, 3 = m), pictured as a brass nameplate on a corporate skyscraper. The 15% profit margin became "tail" (1 = t/d, 5 = l), visualized as a loyal dog wagging its tail exactly 15 times. The 8% market share became "foe" (8 = f/v), imagined as a masked competitor lurking through the marketplace—symbolizing their competition.

But Marcus soon learned that translating numbers into images was only the beginning. To recall full data stories, he began chaining the images into scenes. For example, the product's narrative began with a nameplate on a building ("name"), where a dog wagged its tail ("tail") while chasing a masked intruder ("foe"). This method allowed him to mentally walk through an entire performance report, image by image, number by number.

Detective 369 emphasized the importance of customizing the system. For instance, Marcus treated the percent sign as a visual cue–not part of the Major System itself, but a stylistic enhancer. He imagined a dog's tail branded with a large % sign for "tail-percent," adding context to the image. Decimal points became dramatic punctuation–visual breaks that helped divide multi-part numbers into smaller, imageable chunks.

The technique even extended to competitive intelligence. Marcus encoded market share data from rival firms: Company X had 12% (1 = t/d, 2 = n) = "tin," visualized as a tin can rolling through the market. Company Y held 8% = "foe" (8 = f/v), represented as a masked rival clashing with the tin can. These stories made his team's strategic discussions more vivid and memorable.

The Lifelong Learner Detective: Personal Knowledge Systems

Detective 369's third case study features Elena, a retired teacher who had decided to pursue her lifelong dream of learning Mandarin Chinese. The traditional approach to memorizing Chinese characters and their pronunciations had left her feeling frustrated and discouraged. But when Detective 369 taught her to apply the Major System to language learning, her progress accelerated dramatically.

Elena's breakthrough came when she learned to use the Major System to memorize the numerical tones that are crucial to Mandarin pronunciation. Chinese is a tonal language where the same syllable can have completely different meanings depending on the pitch pattern used. Traditional tone memorization relies on abstract symbols and audio repetition, but Elena learned to convert tone patterns into memorable numerical sequences using the Major System.

The Chinese word "ma" can mean "mother" (tone 1), "hemp" (tone 2), "horse" (tone 3), or "to scold" (tone 4), depending on the tone used. Elena converted these tone numbers into memorable images: tone 1 became "tie" (1), tone 2 became "knee" (2), tone 3 became "me" (3), and tone 4 became "rye" (4). She then created memorable scenes where a mother was adjusting her tie, hemp was wrapped around someone's knee, a horse was pointing at itself saying "me," and someone was scolding while holding rye bread.

The system proved even more powerful for memorizing Chinese phone numbers, addresses, and numerical expressions. Chinese phone numbers follow different patterns than American numbers, but Elena could apply the same Major System principles to create memorable images for any numerical sequence. A Beijing phone number became a narrative about shopping in a Chinese market, with each digit converted to an image that reflected local culture and customs.

Elena also discovered that the Major System enhanced her understanding of Chinese number-related idioms and expressions. The phrase "three three two two" (meaning "scattered" or "in small groups") became "me me no no" in her system, creating a memorable scene where people were saying "me me no no" while scattering in different directions. These cultural connections made the language more meaningful and memorable.

Detective 369 emphasized that Elena's success came from understanding how to adapt the Major System to the unique challenges of language learning. Different languages have different numerical patterns, different cultural associations with numbers, and different ways of expressing numerical concepts. The Major System's flexibility allowed Elena to create a personalized approach that reflected both her learning style and the specific requirements of Mandarin Chinese.

The system also proved valuable for memorizing vocabulary through numerical associations. Chinese character stroke counts, pronunciation guide numbers, and lesson reference numbers all became part of Elena's comprehensive learning system. When she needed to remember that a specific character had 12 strokes, she could instantly visualize "tin" (12) and create a memorable connection between the character's meaning and the image of a tin can.

The Advanced Techniques: Mastering Complex Numerical Sequences

Detective 369 walks to a locked cabinet and withdraws a folder marked "Advanced Protocols." These are the sophisticated techniques that separate expert practitioners from novices–the methods that allow you to handle the most challenging numerical sequences with confidence and precision. Mastering these advanced applications requires understanding not just the basic digit-to-sound mappings, but how to orchestrate multiple techniques in concert.

1. Narrative Chaining: Instead of converting isolated numbers to isolated images, you create continuous stories where each numerical element leads naturally to the next. This approach is particularly powerful for memorizing long sequences like credit card numbers, social security numbers, or complex identification codes.

Detective 369 demonstrates this technique with a 16-digit credit card number: 4532-1458-7963-2841. Rather than memorizing this as separate 4-digit chunks, he converts it to a flowing narrative. The number 4532 becomes "realm" (45) and "mine" (32), creating the opening scene of a story set in a magical realm where miners are excavating precious gems. The number 1458 becomes "trail" (14) and "life" (58), continuing the story as the miners follow a trail that leads to the fountain of life.

The sequence 7963 becomes "beggar" (79) and "jam" (63), adding a character who appears at the fountain–a beggar covered in sticky jam who guards the magical waters. The final sequence 2841 becomes "knife" (28) and "rat" (41), concluding the story as the beggar uses a knife to fight off a giant rat that threatens the fountain. The entire credit card number becomes a memorable fantasy adventure that can be recalled by mentally playing the story from beginning to end.

2. Contextual Encoding: Detective 369 adapts his number-word choices to match the specific context of the information being memorized. Different types of numbers require different approaches to create the most memorable associations. Historical dates might be best encoded with words that relate to the historical period, while phone numbers might use words that relate to the person or business being called.

When memorizing historical dates, Detective 369 chooses words that evoke the appropriate time period. The year 1776 becomes "duck" (17) and "cash" (76), but he visualizes a colonial duck wearing a tricorn hat and carrying a purse full of colonial-era coins. The year 1945 becomes "paper" (19) and "role" (45), but he envisions wartime newspapers and the changing roles of women in society. The contextual connection makes the dates more meaningful and more memorable.

For phone numbers, Detective 369 adapts his word choices to reflect the relationship or business context. A doctor's phone number might use medical-related imagery, while a restaurant's number might involve food-related scenes. This contextual approach creates stronger associations and makes the numbers more personally meaningful.

3. Hierarchical Organization: Detective 369 creates structured systems for managing large collections of numbers. Instead of treating each number as an isolated item, he organizes them into logical hierarchies that reflect their relationships and importance. This approach is particularly valuable for professionals who need to memorize extensive numerical databases.

Detective 369 demonstrates this technique with a system for memorizing case file numbers. Primary case numbers are encoded with particularly vivid imagery and placed in prominent locations within his Memory Palace. Secondary case numbers use less dramatic imagery and are placed in supporting locations. Related case numbers are linked through narrative connections that show their relationships. The entire system creates a comprehensive database that can be navigated efficiently and expanded as needed.

4. Dynamic Updating: Detective 369 maintains and updates his numerical memory systems as information changes. Numbers aren't static—phone numbers change, addresses are updated, financial figures fluctuate. Advanced practitioners develop systems for efficiently updating their mental databases without losing the organizational structure they've built.

Detective 369 has developed protocols for handling these updates that maintain the integrity of his memory systems. When a phone number changes, he doesn't just memorize the new number–he creates a narrative connection showing how the old number transformed into the new one. This approach preserves the investment made in the original memorization while accommodating the new information.

The Field Assignment: Cracking Your First Numerical Case

Detective 369 closes the advanced techniques folder and turns his attention to you. This isn't just theory–it's a practical system that requires hands-on investigation to master. Your mission, should you choose to accept it, is to crack your first numerical case using the Major System, proving to yourself that you can transform cold digits into unforgettable mental imagery.

Your assignment consists of three levels of increasing difficulty, each designed to test different aspects of your Major System skills. Success at each level builds the foundation for the next, creating a comprehensive understanding of how this powerful technique works in practice.

Level One: Basic Cipher Mastery

Your first challenge is to memorize a 12-digit sequence that represents a complex case file number: 471-936-258-047. This sequence contains all the elements that make numbers challenging: multiple digits, various sound combinations, and no obvious pattern. But with the Major System, this seemingly impossible task becomes a manageable creative exercise.

Begin by converting each three-digit group into memorable words using the digit-to-sound mappings. The sequence 471 becomes R (4), K (7), and T (1), which could form "rocket" or "racket." Choose the word that creates the most vivid image for you. The sequence 936 becomes P (9), M (3), and J (6), which could become "pamphlet" or "pomegranate." Again, choose the option that sparks your imagination.

Continue this process for 258, which becomes N (2), L (5), and F (8), possibly forming "knife" or "napalm." The final sequence 047 becomes S (0), R (4), and K (7), which could become "shark" or "spark." Once you have four memorable words, create a single narrative that connects them in sequence.

Detective 369 emphasizes that your story should violate normal physics and logic. If your words are "rocket," "pomegranate," "knife," and "shark," create a scene where a rocket filled with exploding pomegranates crashes into a giant knife, which then transforms into a mechanical shark. The more impossible and dramatic the scene, the more memorable it becomes.

Practice recalling this sequence until you can do it flawlessly without referring to your notes. The goal isn't just to remember the numbers–it's to prove to yourself that the Major System can transform any numerical sequence into memorable imagery.

Level Two: Real-World Application

Your second challenge involves memorizing information that you'll actually use in your daily life. Choose three pieces of numerical information that are important to you: a phone number you need to remember, a significant date, and a numerical code (like a lock combination or account number). Apply the Major System to each piece of information, creating a personalized memory system that serves your actual needs.

For the phone number, break it into manageable chunks and convert each chunk to memorable imagery. Create a story that connects to the person or business associated with the number. If it's a restaurant, incorporate food imagery. If it's a medical office, include health-related elements. The contextual connections make the memory more meaningful and durable.

For the significant date, convert the numbers to images that relate to the event being commemorated. A birthday might use celebratory imagery, while a historical date might incorporate period-appropriate elements. The goal is to create associations that enhance your understanding of the date's significance.

For the numerical code, create a dramatic action sequence where each number-image performs a specific function. A lock combination might become a story about unlocking a treasure chest, with each digit representing a different key or mechanism. The narrative approach makes the sequence easier to remember and more engaging to practice.

Detective 369 emphasizes that real-world application is where the Major System proves its value. These aren't just memory exercises–they're practical tools that can enhance your daily life by reducing dependence on external memory aids.

Level Three: Advanced Integration

Your final challenge involves combining the Major System with other memory techniques you've learned. Create a comprehensive system for memorizing a complex dataset that includes both numerical and non-numerical information. This might involve memorizing a list of historical events with their dates, a set of contacts with their phone numbers, or a collection of financial data with multiple metrics.

Begin by organizing your information into logical categories. Use your Memory Palace to create dedicated areas for different types of data. Apply the Major System to convert all numerical information into memorable imagery. Use the Linking Method to create connections between related items. Employ Active Recall to test your mastery of the complete system.

The goal of this final challenge is to demonstrate that the Major System doesn't exist in isolation–it's part of a comprehensive memory toolkit that becomes more powerful when techniques are combined. Detective 369 has achieved mastery by understanding how different methods complement each other, creating synergistic effects that exceed the sum of their parts.

Practice your integrated system until you can navigate it flawlessly. Test yourself on random access (can you retrieve any piece of information without going through the entire sequence?) and stress testing (can you maintain accuracy when tired or distracted?). The system should feel natural and automatic, not forced or artificial.

The Master Detective's Revelation: Why Numbers Surrender to Images

Detective 369 stands at his window, looking out at the city lights that flicker like neurons in the vast network of human memory. The Major System, he reflects, represents more than just a clever memory trick–it's a fundamental insight into how the human mind processes and stores information. Understanding why this system works so effectively reveals deeper truths about memory, learning, and the nature of human cognition.

The power of the Major System lies in its ability to transform abstract information into concrete experience. Numbers, in their raw form, are among the most difficult types of information for the human brain to process and remember. They don't engage our visual processing systems, they don't connect to our emotional centers, and they don't link to our existing knowledge networks. They exist in a kind of cognitive limbo, recognized but not truly understood.

But when Detective 369 converts numbers to images through the Major System, he's activating multiple memory systems simultaneously. The visual imagery engages the brain's powerful visual processing networks, which evolved to help our ancestors navigate complex environments and recognize important objects. The narrative structure activates our natural storytelling abilities, connecting information through cause-and-effect relationships that make sequences memorable. The emotional content–the drama, surprise, and absurdity–triggers the amygdala, which enhances memory consolidation by marking information as significant.

Research in cognitive neuroscience has consistently shown that information processed through multiple channels is more durable and accessible than information processed through single channels. The Major System leverages this principle by encoding numerical information in verbal, visual, spatial, and emotional formats simultaneously. The result is a memory trace that's far more robust than what traditional numerical memorization can achieve.

Detective 369 has also discovered that the Major System enhances numerical understanding, not just numerical memory. When you convert numbers to images and organize those images into stories, you're creating meaningful relationships between numerical concepts. Mathematical operations become transformations of imagery, statistical relationships become narrative connections, and abstract quantities become concrete experiences.

The system also addresses one of the fundamental challenges of numerical memory: the lack of natural organization. Random numbers have no inherent structure that the mind can grasp, making them difficult to chunk and organize. But the Major System imposes a meaningful structure by converting numbers to words, words to images, and images to stories. This artificial organization becomes a scaffold that supports memory and makes numerical information more manageable.

Perhaps most importantly, the Major System gives you ownership of your numerical memory. Instead of being at the mercy of arbitrary digits, you become the director of memorable mental movies. You choose the images, you craft the stories, and you control the associations. This sense of agency and creativity transforms numerical memorization from a chore into an art form.

Detective 369 has seen this transformation in countless students, professionals, and lifelong learners. They don't just become better at memorizing numbers–they become more confident in their ability to handle numerical information, more creative in their problem-solving approaches, and more sophisticated in their understanding of how memory works.

The Investigation Continues: Building Your Numerical Empire

Detective 369 turns from the window and walks toward the door, his investigation complete but his work far from finished. The Major System, he explains, is both a destination and a journey. You can use it immediately to solve specific numerical challenges, but its true power emerges over time as you build larger and more sophisticated systems.

Your first applications will be modest–perhaps a phone number or a date that you need to remember. But as your skills develop, you'll find yourself creating vast mental databases where thousands of numbers are instantly accessible through vivid imagery. The technique scales beautifully, growing with your ambitions and adapting to your changing needs.

The key to long-term success with the Major System is consistency and patience. Detective 369 has been refining his approach for decades, and he's still discovering new applications and improvements. Start with simple numbers, master the basic digit-to-sound mappings, and let your system evolve organically as your understanding deepens.

Remember that the Major System is ultimately a tool for freedom. Freedom from the anxiety of forgetting important numbers, freedom from dependence on external memory aids, and freedom to engage with numerical information confidently and creatively. It's a tool that serves you rather than controlling you, a system that enhances your natural abilities rather than replacing them.

Detective 369 pauses at the threshold, his hand on the brass doorknob. The fog outside has begun to lift, revealing the clear outline of the city below. Similarly, the fog of confusion that surrounds numerical memory begins to clear when you master the Major System. Numbers are no longer mysterious enemies–they're allies in the grand investigation of learning and memory.

The detective tips his fedora and steps into the morning light. Your numerical cipher is cracked, your phonetic decoder ring is ready, and the techniques for transforming digits into images are now in your hands. The investigation into advanced memory techniques continues, but you're no longer just an observer–you're a participant, a codebreaker, a master of numerical memory.

The numbers that once slipped away like suspects in the night now stand ready to be captured, converted, and committed to memory. Detective 369 has shown you the code, taught you the cipher, and revealed the secrets of numerical mastery. The case files are open, the evidence is clear, and the investigation continues.

The seventh case file closes with the soft click of a combination lock engaging. Detective 369 has revealed the secrets of the Major System–the technique that transforms cold numbers into vivid imagery, abstract digits into concrete memories, and numerical chaos into ordered understanding. The code is cracked, the cipher is mastered, and the investigation continues toward the advanced 100-PEG System.

The Major System is a flexible and powerful tool. But when the case grows more complex—when you're juggling dozens or hundreds of data points—something more structured is required.

Chapter 9: The 100-Peg System - Mastering 00 99

Detective 369 stands before the most impressive evidence wall he's ever constructed—a massive grid containing one hundred distinct slots, each one numbered from 00 to 99. The fluorescent lights cast harsh shadows across the organized chaos of his complete numerical arsenal. Tonight, he faces his most challenging case yet: a criminal network so vast and complex that it requires tracking hundreds of individual data points, each one crucial to cracking the case. This is no job for the simple 26-letter filing system. This calls for the ultimate weapon in the memory detective's arsenal: the 100-Peg System.

There comes a moment in every detective's career when the cases grow beyond the scope of traditional methods. When the suspects multiply into the dozens, when the evidence spans multiple crime scenes, when the timeline stretches across months or even years of criminal activity. Twenty-six alphabetical filing slots simply won't suffice. Even the most elegant Memory Palace can become cluttered and confusing when asked to hold hundreds of discrete pieces of information in perfect order.

Detective 369 has encountered these mega-cases before–complex financial fraud schemes involving dozens of co-conspirators, murder investigations spanning multiple jurisdictions, organized crime networks with intricate hierarchies and relationships. These cases demand a memory system that can handle not just large volumes of information, but precise positioning and instant access to any piece of data, no matter how deeply buried in the investigative web.

The 100-Peg System represents the pinnacle of numerical memory architecture. It's not just a bigger filing cabinet–it's a complete mental database where every number from 00 to 99 becomes a living, breathing character in an ongoing narrative. Once mastered, this system transforms the detective's mind into a precision instrument capable of storing, organizing, and retrieving hundreds of facts with the accuracy of a supercomputer and the speed of intuition.

The Evidence Room: Building Your Number-Word Arsenal

Detective 369 leads you to a room lined with filing cabinets, each drawer carefully labeled with numerical ranges. This is his evidence room for the Major System–a comprehensive collection of number-word pairs that he's developed over decades of investigation. Building this arsenal, he explains, is crucial for mastering the system and achieving the kind of instant recall that separates professionals from amateurs.

The foundation of Detective 369's system is a carefully curated list of words for the numbers 00 through 99. These aren't random selections–each word has been chosen for its visual impact, emotional resonance, and ability to create memorable imagery. The word for 00 is "sauce," creating an immediate image of liquid pouring from a bottle. The word for 01 is "suit," evoking the image of formal business attire. The word for 02 is "sun," bringing to mind the blazing star that dominates our sky.

Each number-word pair serves as a building block for more complex numerical sequences. When Detective 369 needs to remember a longer number, he breaks it into two-digit chunks and converts each chunk to its corresponding word. The number 3247 becomes "moon" (32) and "rock" (47), creating a memorable scene where a massive moon crashes into a rocky cliff with tremendous force.

Detective 369 emphasizes that consistency is crucial in building your number-word arsenal. Once you've chosen a word for a specific number, you should use that same word every time you encounter that number. This consistency creates automatic associations that make the system faster and more reliable. If 23 is "name" in your system, it should always be "name," never "gnome" or "numb," even though these alternatives would be phonetically correct.

The selection of words for your arsenal should prioritize vivid, concrete nouns over abstract concepts. Detective 369 prefers words that create immediate mental images: "tree" rather than "idea," "fire" rather than "hope," "snake" rather than "success." Concrete images are easier to visualize, easier to re-member, and easier to combine into memorable scenes.

Detective 369 also recommends choosing words that naturally lend them-selves to action. Instead of "table" for 15, he might prefer "tile," which can be thrown, shattered, or arranged in patterns. Instead of "sale" for 05, he might choose "seal," which can swim, bark, or balance a ball on its nose. Action-oriented words create more dynamic mental movies, and dynamic scenes are more memorable than static images.

The emotional content of your word choices also matters. Detective 369 has learned that words with strong emotional associations–whether positive or negative–create more durable memories. A word like "cake" (77) brings joy and celebration, while "knife" (28) creates tension and danger. Both emotions serve memory equally well, as long as they create strong mental impressions.

Building your complete 00-99 arsenal takes time and deliberate practice. Detective 369 recommends starting with the most common numbers in your daily life–birthdays, addresses, phone numbers–and gradually expanding your vocabulary. Practice converting random numbers to words until the process becomes automatic. The investment of time required to build this foundation pays dividends for decades of enhanced numerical memory.

Detective 369 also suggests creating personal connections whenever possible. If 47 could be either "rock" or "rug," choose the one that connects to your personal experience. If you're a geologist, "rock" might be more meaningful. If you're an interior designer, "rug" might create stronger associations. Personal relevance makes the system more memorable and more enjoyable to use.

The ultimate goal is to reach the point where seeing any two-digit number immediately triggers its corresponding word without conscious translation. Detective 369 has achieved this level of fluency through years of practice, and he can now convert any number into words as quickly as he can read the digits. This automaticity is what makes the **100-Peg System** so powerful for real-world applications.

The Complete Arsenal: Understanding the 100-Peg Architecture

Detective 369 walks slowly along the length of his evidence wall, his fingers trailing across each numbered slot. The 100-Peg System, he explains, represents the natural evolution of everything he's taught about memory work. It builds directly upon the Major System's phonetic foundation, but instead of generating words on the fly, it creates a permanent, memorized vocabulary of one hundred distinct images, each corresponding to a specific number from 00 to 99.

The genius of this approach lies in its combination of systematic structure with creative flexibility. Where the Major System requires you to convert numbers to sounds to words each time you encounter them, the 100-Peg System front-loads this work. You invest the time once to memorize a comprehensive set of peg images, and then you have instant access to vivid, memorable hooks for any two-digit number you encounter.

Detective 369 demonstrates this principle by pointing to slot 42 on his evidence wall. The number 42, according to the Major System's phonetic rules, converts to the sounds R (4) and N (2). Following these sound patterns, 42 becomes "rain"–not just any rain, but Detective 369's specific, carefully chosen image of a torrential downpour during a nighttime stakeout, complete with the sound of water drumming against car windows and the smell of wet asphalt. This image is so vivid, so personally meaningful, that it appears in his mind instantly whenever he encounters the number 42.

The power of this pre-memorized approach becomes evident when handling complex numerical sequences. Instead of pausing to convert each number through the phonetic system, Detective 369 can instantly visualize a series of images that tell a complete story. The phone number 42-67-31 becomes a narrative where rain (42) falls on a chalk-covered blackboard (67) while a moth (31) flutters frantically around a streetlight. The sequence isn't just remembered–it's experienced as a coherent scene that plays like a movie in the detective's mind.

Each peg image in Detective 369's system has been carefully selected for maximum memorability and minimum confusion. The images are concrete rather than abstract, emotionally neutral rather than charged, and distinctly different from each other to prevent mental interference. Rain doesn't just represent wetness–it represents the specific wetness of that particular downpour, complete with sensory details that make it impossible to confuse with any other weather-related image in the system.

The Database Construction: Building Your Mental Mainframe

Detective 369 opens a thick manual labeled "System Construction Protocols" and spreads detailed charts across his desk. Building a 100-Peg System, he explains, is like constructing a mental mainframe computer–it requires systematic planning, careful attention to detail, and a significant upfront investment of time and effort. But once constructed, this system becomes the most powerful information storage and retrieval tool in the detective's arsenal.

The construction process begins with the systematic application of Major System principles to every number from 00 to 99. Detective 369 demonstrates this process by working through several examples, showing how the phonetic rules transform abstract numbers into concrete, memorable images. The number 00 follows the pattern of S (0) and S (0), which can become "sauce," "sos," or "sassy." Detective 369 chose "sauce" for his system, visualizing a thick, red marinara sauce pouring from a bottle with dramatic slowness.

The number 01 combines S (0) with T or D (1), creating possibilities like "suit," "seed," or "soot." Detective 369 selected "suit," imagining a perfectly pressed business suit hanging in a closet, complete with a crisp white shirt and conservative tie. The formality of the suit creates a strong contrast with the casual messiness of the sauce, ensuring that the two images remain distinct in his mental database.

Each subsequent number receives the same careful treatment. The number 02 becomes "sun," visualized as a blazing yellow orb in a cloudless sky. The number 03 becomes "sum," represented by a chalkboard covered with mathematical equations. The number 04 becomes "sore," depicted as a bandaged wound that throbs with each heartbeat. Detective 369 continues this process through all one hundred numbers, creating a complete vocabulary of images that covers every possible two-digit combination.

The key to effective construction lies in maintaining consistency while ensuring distinctiveness. Detective 369 emphasizes that once you've chosen an image for a specific number, that image must remain unchanged throughout your use of the system. The number 42 is always rain, never "run" or "ruin" or any other phonetically similar word. This consistency creates automatic associations that make the system faster and more reliable with each use.

The selection process also requires attention to the visual and emotional characteristics of each image. Detective 369 avoids images that are too similar to each other–he doesn't use both "rain" and "snow" in his system, as they might cause confusion during high-stress recall situations. He also avoids images with strong personal emotions that might interfere with their use as neutral memory hooks. The goal is to create a collection of images that are vivid enough to be memorable but stable enough to serve as reliable anchors for any type of information.

The Precision Instrument: How the System Transforms Information

Detective 369 pulls out a case file marked "Financial Fraud Investigation" and opens it to reveal a complex web of transactions, dates, and account numbers.

This is where the 100-Peg System reveals its true power–not just as a memory aid, but as a precision instrument for organizing and accessing large amounts of numerical information.

The traditional approach to handling this type of case would involve spreadsheets, databases, and constant reference to written materials. But Detective 369 has transformed the entire investigation into a series of vivid mental movies using his 100-Peg System. Transaction amounts, account numbers, dates, and reference codes all become characters in an ongoing narrative that he can access instantly without any external aids.

The process begins with the systematic conversion of each piece of numerical information into its corresponding peg image. A bank account number ending in 73 becomes associated with "comb," which Detective 369 visualizes as an elegant silver comb with intricate engravings. A transaction amount of $1,542 is broken into chunks–15 becomes "tail," 42 becomes "rain"–creating a scene where a dog's tail is wagging frantically in the rain.

But the true genius of the system lies in how these individual images combine to create memorable narratives. Detective 369 doesn't just remember isolated facts–he remembers stories where the silver comb is being used to groom the wet dog's tail, where the rain is falling on the comb's metallic surface, where the dog is chasing the comb through puddles of water. These impossible scenes are so vivid and emotionally engaging that they become unforgettable, even under the stress of courtroom testimony or high-pressure interrogation.

The system also accommodates the hierarchical nature of complex information. Major categories of evidence receive prominent peg positions–01 through 10 might be reserved for primary suspects, 11 through 20 for key witnesses, 21 through 30 for crucial pieces of physical evidence. Within each category, subcategories can be organized using the remaining peg positions, creating a nested structure that mirrors the logical organization of the investigation.

Detective 369 demonstrates this hierarchical approach with his current case. Suspect number 01 (suit) is the alleged mastermind, visualized as a man in an expensive business suit with briefcases full of cash. Suspect number 02 (sun) is the money laundering specialist, depicted as a figure made of pure golden light who transforms dirty money into clean bills. Suspect number 03 (sum) is the accountant, represented by a human calculator with numbers constantly scrolling across its face.

Each suspect's associated information is then organized using additional peg positions. Suspect 01's bank account information is filed under peg 41 (rat), creating a scene where the suited man is feeding stacks of cash to a giant rat. His home address is encoded using peg 51 (lot), visualized as the suited man standing in an empty lot while wearing his signature business attire. The system creates a web of interconnected images that makes every piece of information accessible through multiple pathways.

The Student Detective: Academic Applications of the Complete System

Detective 369 opens a file marked "Academic Investigations" and reveals how students can harness the 100-Peg System to master even the most challenging academic subjects. The system's ability to handle large volumes of information while maintaining perfect organization makes it ideal for comprehensive exam preparation, research projects, and long-term knowledge building.

Consider Maria, a medical student preparing for her anatomy finals. Traditional study methods had left her overwhelmed by the sheer volume of information–hundreds of bone names, muscle groups, organ systems, and physiological processes that needed to be memorized with perfect accuracy. Detective 369 taught her to transform this medical knowledge into a comprehensive 100-Peg System that turned her textbook into a vivid mental movie.

Maria's transformation began with the systematic organization of anatomical information into numbered categories. The skeletal system occupied peg positions **01-15**, with each bone receiving its own dedicated image. The skull became associated with peg 01 (suit), visualized as a business suit worn by a skeleton, the fabric draped elegantly over the bone structure. The femur connected to peg **02** (sun), depicted as a massive leg bone that glowed with inner light like a miniature sun.

The muscular system filled positions 16-35, with major muscle groups receiving their own peg assignments. The biceps muscle linked to peg 16 (dish), creating a scene where a flexed arm was holding a dinner plate, demonstrating the muscle's function through the action of lifting. The quadriceps connected to peg 17 (tack), visualized as four metal tacks driven into the front of the thigh, representing the four heads of the quadriceps muscle.

Maria's system continued through all major body systems, with the cardiovascular system occupying positions 36-50, the respiratory system filling slots 51-65, and the nervous system taking up positions 66-80. Each system received comprehensive coverage, with individual organs, functions, and pathologies all receiving their own peg assignments within the broader organizational framework.

The power of this systematic approach became evident during Maria's exam preparation. Instead of frantically reviewing hundreds of pages of notes, she could mentally walk through her 100-Peg System, visiting each image in sequence and reviewing the associated information. When asked about the function of the biceps muscle, she didn't just recall the factual information–she saw the flexed arm holding the dinner plate, complete with the muscle's attachment points and range of motion.

Detective 369 emphasizes that Maria's success came from understanding how to layer detailed information within each peg position. The biceps image didn't just represent the muscle itself–it contained information about muscle origin and insertion points, nerve innervation, blood supply, and common injuries. The dinner plate scene became a comprehensive filing system where different aspects of the muscle were stored in different parts of the image.

The system also accommodated the interconnected nature of anatomical knowledge. When Maria needed to understand how the biceps muscle related to the shoulder joint, she could visualize the connection between peg 16 (dish/biceps) and peg 05 (seal/shoulder), creating a scene where the flexed arm was reaching toward a seal balanced on its shoulder. These cross-references made the information more meaningful and created multiple pathways for retrieval.

The Professional Detective: Corporate Intelligence Applications

Detective 369 opens another case file, this one marked "Corporate Intelligence Operations," and reveals how business professionals can deploy the 100-Peg System to master the complex information landscapes of modern workplaces. In professional environments where success depends on instant access to vast amounts of data, the system becomes an invaluable competitive advantage.

Consider David, a senior sales manager responsible for a product portfolio containing 85 different items, each with multiple specifications, pricing tiers, and competitive positioning details. Traditional approaches–spreadsheets, product catalogs, and reference materials–left him dependent on external tools and vulnerable to information gaps during crucial client meetings. Detective 369 taught him to transform his entire product knowledge into a comprehensive 100-Peg System that made him the most informed person in any sales situation.

David's transformation began with the systematic assignment of each product to a specific peg position. Products were organized by category and importance, with flagship items receiving prominent positions in the 01-20 range, secondary products occupying positions 21-40, and specialized items filling the remaining slots. Each product received its own unique peg image that captured both its position in the system and its essential characteristics.

Product 01 (suit) was their premium enterprise software solution, visualized as a business executive wearing an expensive suit made entirely of computer code, the fabric shimmering with flowing data streams. Product 02 (sun) was their cloud-based platform, depicted as a brilliant sun composed of interconnected servers, radiating connectivity and power. Product 03 (sum) was their analytics package, represented by a giant calculator that could process infinite amounts of business data.

Each product's associated information was then organized using additional peg positions within David's system. Product 01's pricing structure was filed under peg 51 (lot), creating a scene where the suited executive was standing in a lot filled with money, the bills organized into neat stacks representing different pricing tiers. Technical specifications were stored under peg 61 (sheet), visualized as the executive holding a bedsheet covered with technical diagrams and performance metrics.

The system's power became evident during David's client presentations. When asked about the enterprise software's integration capabilities, he didn't just recite features–he saw the suited executive shaking hands with figures representing various business systems, each handshake creating a visible connection that demonstrated seamless integration. The visual nature of the information made his presentations more engaging and memorable for clients.

Detective 369 emphasizes that David's success came from understanding how to create meaningful connections between numerical positions and business concepts. The system wasn't just a filing cabinet–it was a dynamic network where product information lived in relationship to market conditions, client needs, and competitive landscape. When a client expressed interest in a particular feature, David could instantly visualize how that feature connected to other products in his portfolio, creating opportunities for cross-selling and solution development.

The system also accommodated the dynamic nature of business information. When product specifications changed, David didn't need to relearn everything–he simply updated the relevant section of his existing mental image. When new products were added to the portfolio, they were integrated into the existing framework rather than creating entirely new memory structures. This flexibility made the system practical for long-term professional development.

The Lifelong Learner Detective: Personal Knowledge Systems

Detective 369 opens his final case file, marked "Personal Knowledge Development," which contains some of his most meaningful work–helping individuals organize and master information that enriches their personal lives and intellectual pursuits. The 100-Peg System's capacity for comprehensive organization makes it ideal for lifelong learning projects that span multiple subjects and years of study.

Consider Elena, a retired engineer who had decided to pursue her passion for art history. The traditional approach to learning about art–museum visits, textbooks, and lecture series–had left her struggling to remember the relationships between different artists, movements, and historical periods. Detective 369 taught her to create a comprehensive 100-Peg System that transformed art history into a vivid mental gallery where every piece of information had its proper place.

Elena's transformation began with the systematic organization of art history into chronological and thematic categories. The Renaissance period occupied peg positions 01-15, with major artists receiving their own dedicated slots. Leonardo da Vinci connected to peg 01 (suit), visualized as the master artist wearing a business suit while painting the Mona Lisa, the anachronistic clothing creating a memorable contrast with the historical setting. Michelangelo linked to peg 02 (sun), depicted as the sculptor working on David while surrounded by blazing sunlight that illuminated every muscle and detail of the marble figure.

The Baroque period filled positions 16-30, with artists like Caravaggio and Rubens receiving their own peg assignments. Caravaggio connected to peg 16 (dish), visualized as the artist painting dramatic chiaroscuro effects on the surface of a dinner plate, the stark contrasts of light and shadow creating the characteristic drama of Baroque composition. Rubens linked to peg 17 (tack), depicted as the artist using metal tacks to pin voluptuous figures to his canvas, representing his famous full-figured subjects.

Elena's system continued through all major art periods, with Impressionism occupying positions 31-45, Modern Art filling slots 46-60, and Contemporary Art taking up positions 61-75. Each period received comprehensive coverage, with individual artists, techniques, and masterpieces all receiving their own peg assignments within the broader organizational framework.

The power of this systematic approach became evident during Elena's museum visits. Instead of consulting guidebooks or audio tours, she could mentally walk through her 100-Peg System, instantly accessing information about any artwork she encountered. When viewing a Van Gogh painting, she didn't just see brushstrokes and color–she saw peg 32 (moon), her chosen image for Van Gogh, depicted as the artist painting swirling moons and stars that moved with the same energy as his distinctive style.

Detective 369 emphasizes that Elena's success came from understanding how to create personally meaningful connections between numerical positions and artistic concepts. The system wasn't just about memorizing facts–it was about building a comprehensive understanding of how art evolved through time, how different movements influenced each other, and how individual artists contributed to the broader cultural conversation.

The system also accommodated Elena's expanding interests and deepening knowledge. When she discovered a new artist or learned about a previously unknown technique, the information could be easily integrated into her existing framework. When she wanted to explore connections between different periods or movements, she could visualize the relationships between different peg positions, creating a dynamic network of artistic knowledge that supported both learning and creative thinking.

The Advanced Deployment: Master-Level Applications

Detective 369 walks to a specialized cabinet marked "Elite Operations" and withdraws a folder containing his most sophisticated applications of the 100-Peg System. These techniques represent the pinnacle of numerical memory mastery, approaches that allow expert practitioners to handle extraordinarily complex information with precision and efficiency.

1. Nested Peg Systems: Instead of using each peg position for a single piece of information, master practitioners create sub-systems within each peg, exponentially increasing the system's capacity. Peg 01 doesn't just hold one item—it becomes a complete filing system with its own internal organization. This allows a single 100-Peg System to accommodate thousands of discrete pieces of information while maintaining perfect organization.

Detective 369 demonstrates this technique using his investigation of a major embezzlement case. Peg 01 (suit) doesn't just represent the primary suspect—it contains an entire dossier organized within the suit image itself. The suit's jacket holds personal information, the pants contain financial records, the shirt stores communication logs, and the tie holds evidence of criminal activity. Each section of the suit becomes a sub-peg with its own detailed information, creating a hierarchical structure that can accommodate vast amounts of data.

2. Dynamic Peg Linking: Detective 369 creates systematic connections between different peg positions to reflect real-world relationships. Information rarely exists in isolation—facts relate to other facts, events influence other events, and understanding emerges from seeing these connections. Advanced practitioners use their peg images to create visible relationships that mirror the logical structure of their information.

Detective 369 illustrates this technique by showing how his embezzlement case pegs connect to each other through impossible but memorable actions. The suited figure from peg 01 is shown shaking hands with the sun figure from peg 02, their interaction creating a visible connection that represents the collaboration between two suspects. The sun figure then passes documents to the sum figure from peg 03, showing how the money laundering specialist worked with the accountant to hide the stolen funds.

3. Contextual Peg Adaptation: Detective 369 adjusts his peg images to match the specific requirements of different information types. The same peg image might appear differently when filing scientific data versus historical facts versus personal memories. The suit from peg 01 retains its essential character while adapting its appearance to enhance the memorability of specific information types.

These advanced techniques require significant practice and systematic development, but they transform the 100-Peg System from a simple organizational tool into a sophisticated information management system capable of handling professional-level complexity while maintaining the accessibility that makes the basic system so effective.

The Master Class: Advanced Integration Strategies

Detective 369 opens his final training manual, marked "Integration Protocols," and reveals how the 100-Peg System achieves its ultimate power through combination with other memory techniques. The system doesn't exist in isolation—it becomes exponentially more effective when layered with the spatial organization of Memory Palaces, the narrative flow of Linking Methods, and the systematic review of Spaced Repetition.

The most powerful integration combines the 100-Peg System with the Memory Palace technique. Detective 369 has created a vast mental complex where each peg image has its own dedicated location within a familiar building. Peg 01 (suit) resides in the executive office, peg 02 (sun) illuminates the conference room, peg 03 (sum) operates from the accounting department. This spatial organization provides multiple pathways to the same information, making retrieval faster and more reliable.

The integration with Linking Methods creates dynamic narratives that connect related information through cause-and-effect relationships. Instead of storing isolated facts, Detective 369 creates stories where peg images interact, influence each other, and participate in ongoing dramas that make entire information networks memorable. The embezzlement case becomes a crime thriller where the suited executive, the glowing sun, and the calculating sum engage in an elaborate scheme that unfolds through multiple acts and scenes.

The combination with Spaced Repetition ensures that the 100-Peg System remains sharp and accessible over time. Detective 369 has developed systematic review protocols that test his peg images at strategic intervals, reinforcing the associations before they can fade. This maintenance keeps the system operating at peak efficiency, ensuring that information remains instantly accessible even after months or years of storage.

The integration also accommodates cross-referencing between different memory systems. When Detective 369 encounters information that relates to multiple cases or topics, he can create visible connections between his various memory systems. The same peg image might appear in different Memory Palaces, participate in different Linking narratives, and connect to different Alphabet Peg systems, creating a comprehensive network of knowledge that supports both specific recall and general understanding.

The Field Assignment: Constructing Your Complete Arsenal

Detective 369 closes his training materials and turns his attention to you. This isn't just theory–it's a practical system that requires hands-on construction and testing to master. Your mission, should you choose to accept it, is to build and deploy your own 100-Peg System, proving that you can transform any large-scale information challenge into a manageable, organized mental database.

Your assignment consists of three phases, each building upon the previous one to create a comprehensive understanding of how the 100-Peg System works in practice. Success at each phase demonstrates mastery of increasingly sophisticated organizational skills and prepares you for the advanced applications that make this system truly powerful.

Phase One: Building your Numerical Evidence Locker

Your first challenge is to construct your complete 100-Peg System by selecting and memorizing images for all numbers from 00 to 99. This requires systematic application of Major System principles, careful attention to image distinctiveness, and significant practice to achieve automatic recall. Begin by working through the numbers systematically, converting each one to its phonetic sounds and then to a memorable image.

Use the Major System rules to convert each number: 00 becomes S-S sounds, 01 becomes S-T sounds, 02 becomes S-N sounds, and so on through 99 which becomes P-P sounds. For each number,

select an image that creates a vivid mental picture while remaining distinct from all other images in your system. Write down your complete 100-Peg list and practice until you can instantly recall the image for any number called out randomly.

The goal is to achieve the same level of automaticity that Detective 369 has developed–immediate, effortless access to any peg image without conscious effort. This foundation is crucial for all advanced applications of the system.

Phase Two: Information Integration

Your second challenge involves using your 100-Peg System to organize and memorize a substantial collection of information. Choose a subject area that interests you and requires organizing at least 50 distinct pieces of information–this could be historical events, scientific facts, literary works, or professional knowledge. Apply your peg system to create a comprehensive mental database for this information.

For each piece of information, create a memorable association between the fact and its corresponding peg image. Use Detective 369's principles of bizarre, impossible, emotionally engaging connections to make the associations unforgettable. Practice accessing your information through the peg system until you can instantly recall any fact by thinking of its numerical position.

Test your system by having someone else call out random numbers while you immediately recall the associated information. The goal is to demonstrate that numerical organization makes large amounts of information more accessible, not more difficult to remember.

Phase Three: Advanced Integration

Your final challenge involves combining your 100-Peg System with other memory techniques to create a comprehensive information management system. Choose a complex subject that requires sophisticated organization–perhaps a professional knowledge base, academic subject matter, or comprehensive personal interest. Apply your integrated system to organize this information, demonstrating that the 100-Peg System becomes more powerful when combined with other memory techniques.

Use Memory Palace techniques to give your peg images spatial locations, Linking Methods to create narratives between related pegs, and Active Recall protocols to maintain the system over time. Practice navigating your integrated system until it feels natural and efficient, capable of handling the most demanding information challenges you might encounter.

The Master Detective's Revelation: Why Numbers Bow to Images

Detective 369 stands at his window, looking out at the city lights that form patterns like the numerical connections in his vast mental database. The 100-Peg System, he reflects, represents more than just an advanced memory technique–it's a fundamental transformation in how you relate to numerical information and large-scale data management.

The system works because it leverages the brain's natural preferences for concrete, visual, emotionally engaging information over abstract numerical concepts. When you transform numbers into images, you're not just making them easier to remember–you're making them more meaningful, more personally relevant, and more integrated into your existing knowledge networks.

Detective 369 has discovered that the 100-Peg System also enhances understanding, not just memory. When you organize information numerically and connect it through vivid imagery, you're creating systematic knowledge structures that support both recall and analysis. The system doesn't just store facts–it builds frameworks for thinking about complex information in organized, productive ways.

The technique also addresses the scalability challenges that limit other memory systems. While Memory Palaces can become cluttered and Linking Methods can become unwieldy with large amounts of information, the 100-Peg System maintains its effectiveness even when handling hundreds of discrete facts. The numerical organization provides a reliable backbone that supports any amount of information without losing coherence.

Perhaps most importantly, the 100-Peg System creates a sense of mastery over complex information. Instead of feeling overwhelmed by large datasets, you become the director of comprehensive mental databases. You don't just remember information–you organize it, connect it, and make it serve your specific needs and interests.

Detective 369 has seen this transformation in countless students, professionals, and lifelong learners. They don't just become better at memorizing numbers–they become more confident in their ability to handle numerical information, more systematic in their thinking, and more effective in their decision-making. The 100-Peg System isn't just a memory technique–it's a foundation for intellectual empowerment.

The Investigation Continues: Building Your Information Empire

Detective 369 turns from the window and walks toward the door, his investigation complete but his work far from finished. The 100-Peg System, he explains, is both a destination and a journey. You can use it immediately to organize specific information challenges, but its true power emerges over time as you build comprehensive knowledge systems that serve your evolving needs and ambitions.

Your first applications will be modest–perhaps organizing a professional knowledge base or academic subject matter. But as your skills develop, you'll find yourself creating sophisticated information architectures where thousands of facts are instantly accessible through numerical pathways. The technique scales beautifully, growing with your ambitions and adapting to your changing requirements.

The key to long-term success with the 100-Peg System is consistency and systematic development. Detective 369 has been refining his approach for decades, and he's still discovering new applications and improvements. Start with careful construction of your basic peg list, master the fundamental principles, and let your system evolve organically as your understanding deepens.

Remember that the 100-Peg System is ultimately a tool for intellectual freedom. Freedom from the anxiety of information overload, freedom from dependence on external memory aids, and freedom to engage with complex knowledge confidently and systematically. It's a tool that serves you rather than controlling you, a system that enhances your natural abilities rather than replacing them.

Detective 369 pauses at the threshold, his hand on the brass doorknob. The fog outside has begun to lift, revealing the clear outline of the city below. Similarly, the fog of information chaos begins to clear when you master the 100-Peg System. Random numbers become organized knowledge, overwhelming data becomes systematic understanding, and complex information becomes manageable intelligence.

The detective tips his fedora and steps into the morning light. Your complete numerical arsenal is constructed, your 100-Peg System is ready for deployment, and the techniques for comprehensive information mastery are now in your hands. The investigation into memory techniques has reached its systematic conclusion, but your journey toward intellectual mastery is just beginning.

The scattered evidence that once threatened to overwhelm now stands ready to be numbered, organized, and retrieved with numerical precision. Detective 369 has shown you the system, taught you the techniques, and revealed the secrets of large-scale memory management. The complete arsenal is yours, the database is constructed, and the investigation continues toward whatever challenges await in the advanced applications of memory mastery.

Chapter 10: Memory for Business and Leadership

Detective 369 adjusts his tie and steps into the glass-walled boardroom of a Fortune 500 corporation. The mahogany table stretches before him like a battlefield, surrounded by leather chairs that have witnessed countless corporate campaigns. Tonight, he's investigating the most competitive environment on earth: the modern business world, where information is power, relationships are currency, and memory can mean the difference between closing the deal and watching it slip away to a more prepared competitor.

In the shadowy corridors of corporate America, Detective 369 has observed a peculiar phenomenon. While executives invest millions in the latest technology, hire teams of consultants, and deploy sophisticated analytics platforms, they consistently overlook the most powerful competitive weapon of all: a perfectly trained memory. The ability to recall names, numbers, and crucial details without fumbling for notes or consulting devices doesn't just impress clients–it transforms how business gets done.

The detective has spent years infiltrating boardrooms, sales meetings, and executive conferences, studying the habits of the most successful business leaders. What he's discovered would surprise most MBA programs: the executives who rise to the top aren't necessarily the smartest or the most educated. They're the ones who can remember everything that matters, creating an aura of competence and preparation that becomes their ultimate competitive advantage.

Tonight, Detective 369 reveals the secret intelligence techniques that can transform any business professional into a memory master. These aren't just party tricks or academic exercises–they're practical tools for dominating meetings, building stronger relationships, and making decisions with the confidence that comes from having all the facts at your mental fingertips.

The Corporate Crime Scene: Understanding the Memory Challenge

Detective 369 walks slowly around the boardroom table, his trained eye cataloging the evidence of memory failure that litters the corporate landscape. Smartphones clutched desperately in sweaty palms, notebooks overflowing with illegible scrawl, laptops propped open like security blankets–all symptoms of executives who have surrendered their mental sovereignty to external memory aids.

The modern business environment, he explains, is fundamentally a memory challenge disguised as a strategy problem. Every meeting requires you to remember who said what and when. Every presentation demands instant access to facts, figures, and supporting details. Every networking event tests your ability to connect names to faces, companies to industries, and conversations to follow-up actions. Success in business isn't just about having good ideas–it's about having perfect recall of the information needed to execute those ideas effectively.

Detective 369 has documented the specific memory challenges that separate successful executives from the struggling masses. Client information represents the first major category–names, preferences, history, and relationship details that can make or break crucial business relationships. A pharmaceutical sales representative who remembers that Dr. Johnson prefers morning meetings, has two children in college, and expressed concerns about drug interactions in their last conversation doesn't just have an advantage–they have an entirely different relationship with that client.

Financial data forms the second critical category. Revenue figures, profit margins, budget allocations, and competitive benchmarks must be instantly accessible during strategic discussions. Detective 369 has watched executives lose credibility in real-time when they can't recall the basic numbers that drive their business. The CEO who confidently states quarterly results without consulting notes commands respect in a way that no amount of charisma can compensate for.

Strategic information represents the third essential category. Market trends, competitive intelligence, regulatory changes, and industry developments must be organized and accessible for quick retrieval during decision-making conversations. The executive who can instantly connect a proposed strategy to relevant market data, competitive moves, and regulatory constraints demonstrates the kind of comprehensive thinking that boards value and competitors fear.

Operational details form the fourth crucial category. Project timelines, resource allocations, team capabilities, and process improvements require systematic memory organization to manage effectively. The manager who can discuss any project without referring to status reports creates confidence in their ability to execute complex initiatives.

Detective 369 emphasizes that these memory challenges aren't just about convenience–they're about perception and power. In business, being prepared means being respected. The executive who never needs to look anything up develops a reputation for competence that opens doors, wins clients, and accelerates career advancement. Conversely, the leader who constantly fumbles for information loses credibility with every forgotten name and misremembered statistic.

The Intelligence Network: Building Your Business Memory System

Detective 369 opens his briefcase and reveals a sophisticated filing system that would be the envy of any intelligence agency. This is his Business Memory Architecture–a comprehensive framework for organizing and accessing the thousands of pieces of information that drive corporate success. The system combines multiple memory techniques into an integrated platform designed specifically for the demands of executive leadership.

The foundation of this architecture is what Detective 369 calls the *"Corporate Memory Palace"*–a mental headquarters designed around familiar business environments. Unlike the personal Memory Palaces used for academic or personal information, the Corporate Memory Palace is built using office buildings, conference centers, and business locations that reflect the professional context where the information will be used.

Detective 369 demonstrates this principle using the corporate headquarters where he's currently operating. The executive floor becomes his strategic information center, with the CEO's office housing market intelligence, the CFO's office containing financial data, and the boardroom storing competitive analysis. Each office provides dedicated space for specific types of business information, creating natural organizational categories that mirror how executives actually think about their businesses.

The middle floors of his Corporate Memory Palace house operational information. The sales department stores client data, relationship history, and pipeline information. The marketing floor contains campaign details, brand positioning, and customer insights. The operations area holds project time-lines, resource allocations, and process improvements. This spatial organization makes information retrieval intuitive and fast, even under the pressure of high-stakes business situations.

The ground floor serves as Detective 369's networking center, where he files information about business contacts, industry relationships, and social connections. The reception area contains basic contact information, while individual offices house detailed relationship data, personal preferences, and conversation history. This systematic approach to relationship management gives him an enormous advantage in building and maintaining the professional networks that drive business success.

The system also incorporates specialized memory techniques optimized for business applications. The Major System handles all numerical information–financial figures, dates, codes, and statistics that must be recalled with perfect accuracy. Client phone numbers become memorable images, quarterly results transform into vivid scenes, and budget allocations turn into dramatic narratives that make financial planning more engaging and memorable.

The Alphabet PEG System organizes categorical information that doesn't fit neatly into spatial frameworks. Industry classifications, product categories, and strategic initiatives receive alphabetical organization that makes them systematically accessible. This dual organization–spatial for complex information, alphabetical for categorical data–creates redundant pathways that ensure nothing important is ever forgotten.

The Executive Suite: Leadership Memory Applications

Detective 369 walks to the head of the boardroom table and takes the position typically reserved for the CEO. From this vantage point, he explains, the memory challenges facing senior executives become crystal clear. Leadership isn't just about making good decisions–it's about making informed decisions quickly, based on comprehensive recall of relevant information from across the entire organization.

1. **Strategic Situational Awareness:** Effective leaders must maintain mental models of their entire business ecosystem—competitors, customers, suppliers, regulators, and market conditions—that can be accessed instantly during

strategic discussions. This requires a sophisticated memory architecture that connects disparate pieces of information into coherent intelligence networks.

Detective 369 demonstrates this with a case study from his investigation of a successful technology CEO. This executive had created a comprehensive Memory Palace using the layout of a major airport, with different terminals representing different market segments. The domestic terminal housed information about traditional customers, the international terminal contained global expansion data, and the cargo area stored supplier and vendor information. Each gate within these terminals held detailed information about specific companies, relationships, and strategic opportunities.

When board discussions turned to competitive threats, this CEO could mentally walk through the "competitive intelligence terminal" and instantly access detailed information about rival companies. He knew their leadership teams, recent strategic moves, financial performance, and likely future actions. This comprehensive awareness allowed him to speak with authority about competitive positioning and market dynamics without ever consulting external sources.

2. Relationship Intelligence: Business success ultimately depends on relationships, and effective leaders must remember enormous amounts of personal and professional information about the people who matter to their organizations. This includes not just basic contact information, but preferences, history, family details, and relationship dynamics that can make or break important business relationships.

Detective 369 reveals how successful executives use Memory Palace techniques to create comprehensive relationship databases. One pharmaceutical industry leader had transformed his childhood neighborhood into a relationship management system, with different houses representing different customer segments. The house where his best friend lived became the repository for information about his most important clients. The school building housed information about regulatory contacts. The community center stored details about industry colleagues and competitors.

Within each building, individual rooms contained detailed information about specific relationships. The living room held basic contact information and professional background. The kitchen stored personal preferences and family details. The bedroom contained confidential information about business challenges and opportunities. This intimate organization made relationship information feel personal and meaningful, ensuring that important details were never forgotten.

3. Financial Command and Control: Leaders must have instant access to the numerical data that drives business decisions. This includes not just current financial results, but historical trends, budget allocations, competitive benchmarks, and financial projections that inform strategic planning. Memory techniques must make this numerical information as accessible as basic vocabulary.

Detective 369 demonstrates how executives use the Major System to master financial information. Revenue figures, profit margins, and budget allocations become vivid mental images that can be recalled instantly during financial discussions. A quarterly revenue figure of $2.3 million becomes "name" (23) and "sauce" (00), creating a memorable scene where the company's nameplate is dripping with golden sauce, representing profitable performance.

This approach extends to complex financial analysis and strategic planning. Budget allocations across different departments become characters in ongoing narratives. The marketing budget might be represented by an advertising executive covered in colorful paint, while the R&D budget becomes a scientist surrounded by bubbling beakers. These character-based representations make budget discussions more engaging and ensure that financial details are never forgotten.

The Sales Floor: Memory for Revenue Generation

Detective 369 descends to the sales floor, where the memory stakes are highest and the competition most intense. In the world of sales, he explains, memory isn't just a professional advantage–it's the difference between hitting quota and missing targets, between building long-term relationships and being replaced by hungrier competitors.

The sales environment presents unique memory challenges that require specialized techniques and systematic organization. Sales professionals must master vast amounts of product information, maintain detailed knowledge about dozens or hundreds of prospects, and navigate complex competitive landscapes where information advantages translate directly into revenue results.

Detective 369 reveals how top sales performers use Memory Palace techniques to create comprehensive product knowledge systems. One software sales executive had transformed a local shopping mall into a complete product information center. Each store in the mall represented a different software module, with the store's characteristics reflecting the module's functionality. The electronics store housed the analytics package, with its displays showing colorful charts and graphs. The sports store contained the performance monitoring tools, with equipment demonstrating speed and efficiency measurements.

Within each store, different sections held specific product information. The checkout area contained pricing details, the customer service desk housed support information, and the stockroom stored technical specifications. This organized approach ensured that product knowledge was not just memorized but systematically organized for quick retrieval during client presentations.

The prospect management challenge requires even more sophisticated memory techniques. Sales professionals must remember not just contact information, but conversation history, pain points, decision-making processes, and relationship dynamics for dozens of potential clients simultaneously. Traditional CRM systems provide external storage, but the sales professional who can access this information mentally has an enormous advantage during face-to-face meetings.

Detective 369 demonstrates how successful sales professionals create prospect Memory Palaces using familiar business environments. One pharmaceutical sales representative had transformed a medical complex into her prospect management system. Each medical office represented a different client, with the office characteristics reflecting the client's personality and business situation. The pediatrician's office was bright and colorful, matching the doctor's energetic personality. The cardiologist's office was more serious and subdued, reflecting his methodical approach to decision-making.

Within each office, specific locations held detailed prospect information. The waiting room contained basic contact information and practice details. The examination room housed information about current challenges and pain points. The doctor's private office stored decision-making criteria and competitive intelligence. The pharmacy held information about current vendors and contract status.

This systematic approach to prospect organization allowed the sales professional to walk into any meeting with comprehensive mental preparation. She knew not just what products to discuss, but how to position them, what objections to anticipate, and what relationship factors might influence the decision-making process.

The competitive intelligence component requires memory techniques that can handle rapidly changing information about rival companies, products, and sales strategies. Detective 369 has developed specialized approaches for organizing competitive data using linking methods that connect related pieces of information through logical narratives.

Competitive information becomes an ongoing story where different companies are characters in a business drama. Product launches, pricing changes, and strategic moves become plot developments that advance the narrative. This story-based approach makes competitive intelligence more engaging and ensures that important developments are remembered and connected to broader market trends.

The Networking Circuit: Memory for Relationship Building

Detective 369 moves to the company's hospitality suite, where business cards are exchanged like intelligence documents and every conversation could lead to a career-changing opportunity. The networking environment, he explains, represents the ultimate test of social memory–the ability to remember names, faces, companies, and conversation details that can be leveraged into valuable business relationships.

Professional networking presents a perfect storm of memory challenges. Events typically involve meeting dozens of new people in a short time period. Conversations are brief and interrupted. Business cards accumulate faster than they can be processed. The social pressure to appear engaged and interested makes it difficult to focus on memory encoding. Yet the long-term value of these relationships often depends entirely on your ability to remember and follow up on specific conversation details.

Detective 369 reveals the systematic approach that successful networkers use to master these challenges. The foundation is what he calls **the "Event Memory Palace"—a mental mapping** of the networking venue that provides organized storage for relationship information. Before attending any networking event, effective professionals conduct a mental reconnaissance of the location, identifying specific areas where different types of relationship information can be systematically stored.

The entrance area becomes the repository for basic contact information–names, companies, and titles that must be remembered accurately for follow-up purposes. The bar area stores personal information and preferences that can be used to build rapport in future conversations. The main networking area houses business intelligence–company challenges, industry insights, and strategic opportunities that were discussed during initial meetings. The quiet conversation areas hold confidential information and potential collaboration opportunities that require careful handling.

Within each area, specific locations correspond to individual contacts. The corner table by the window might house information about the marketing director from the pharmaceutical company. The space by the hors d'oeuvres station could contain details about the startup founder seeking venture capital. This spatial organization ensures that networking information is not just collected but systematically organized for future reference.

Detective 369 demonstrates how effective networkers use association techniques to connect names with faces and companies. Each person becomes a character in a memorable story that incorporates their name, appearance, and business information. John Smith from Acme Corporation becomes "John the Smith" working at the "peak of achievement" (ACME), with a mental image of a blacksmith hammering metal at the top of a mountain. The more creative and personal these associations, the more likely they are to survive the memory challenges of busy professional schedules.

The conversation content requires specialized linking techniques that connect business information to personal details through memorable narratives. When the pharmaceutical marketing director mentions challenges with regulatory compliance, this information gets linked to her personal story about hiking in Colorado, creating a memorable scene where she's navigating regulatory obstacles like mountain trails. These personal connections make business information more meaningful and easier to recall during follow-up conversations.

The follow-up component is where networking memory techniques prove their value. Detective 369 has observed that most networking efforts fail not because of poor initial connections, but because of inadequate follow-up systems. The professional who can send personalized follow-up messages that reference specific conversation details creates a powerful impression of engagement and interest.

Effective networkers use spaced repetition techniques to maintain relationship information over time. Contact details, conversation history, and relationship development opportunities are reviewed on systematic schedules that prevent important connections from becoming forgotten. This ongoing maintenance ensures that networking investments continue to generate value long after the initial meeting.

The Presentation Platform: Memory for Public Speaking

Detective 369 steps behind the podium at the front of the boardroom, his presence commanding attention even in the empty space. From this position, he explains, the memory challenges facing business presenters become immediately apparent. Effective presentations require not just good content, but the ability to deliver that content with confidence, authority, and engagement that can only come from complete mastery of the material.

The traditional approach to presentation preparation–slides, notes, and teleprompters–undermines the presenter's credibility and effectiveness. Audiences can immediately distinguish between speakers who truly know their material and those who are simply reading prepared remarks. The presenter who can speak without notes, who can access any piece of information instantly, and who can adapt their content dynamically based on audience reactions develops a level of authority that no number of visual aids can provide.

Detective 369 reveals how successful executives use Memory Palace techniques to master presentation content. Instead of memorizing speeches word-for-word, they create spatial journeys through their material that allow for flexible delivery while ensuring comprehensive coverage. The presentation becomes a guided tour through organized information rather than a rigid recitation of prepared remarks.

A technology CEO preparing for a major product launch had transformed the venue for his presentation into a Memory Palace that housed all his content. The stage represented the product overview, with specific areas designated for different features and benefits. The front rows of the audience contained market analysis and competitive positioning. The back of the auditorium housed financial projections and business model information. The side exits held supporting data and backup information that could be accessed if needed.

This spatial organization allowed the CEO to navigate his presentation like a familiar building. He could start with the product overview on stage, move to competitive analysis in the front rows, and conclude with financial projections in the back of the auditorium. If audience questions required additional detail, he could mentally visit the side exits to access supporting information. The entire presentation felt conversational and natural while maintaining comprehensive coverage of complex material.

The question-and-answer component requires specialized memory techniques that can handle unpredictable information requests. Detective 369 has developed approaches that organize supporting information in easily accessible formats that can be retrieved instantly during interactive discussions. Potential questions are anticipated and organized alphabetically, with comprehensive answers stored using linking techniques that ensure complete and accurate responses.

Statistical information and financial data require Major System applications that make numerical information as memorable as narrative content. Revenue projections, market size estimates, and competitive benchmarks become vivid mental images that can be recalled instantly during data-heavy presentations. A market size of $4.7 billion becomes "rock" (47) and "sauce" (00), creating a memorable scene where massive rocks are covered in golden sauce, representing the valuable market opportunity.

The adaptation capability separates truly effective presenters from merely competent ones. Detective 369 has observed that the best business speakers can modify their presentations in real-time based on audience reactions, questions, and energy levels. This requires memory systems that provide flexible access to content rather than rigid sequential organization.

Effective presenters use linking techniques that connect related pieces of information through multiple pathways. The same content can be accessed through different routes depending on the presentation flow. Market analysis might be reached directly from the product overview, or indirectly through competitive positioning, or as supporting information for financial projections. This network organization provides the flexibility needed for dynamic audience engagement.

The Crisis Management Center: Memory Under Pressure

Detective 369 moves to the company's crisis management center, where multiple screens display real-time information feeds and emergency communication protocols. In this high-pressure environment, he explains, memory becomes a survival skill. When organizations face crises–whether competitive threats, regulatory challenges, or operational failures–leaders must access vast amounts of information quickly and accurately while making decisions that could determine the company's future.

Crisis situations present unique memory challenges because they combine enormous information demands with extreme time pressure and emotional stress. Traditional information management approaches break down when there's no time to consult databases, review files, or coordinate with support teams. The leader who can access critical information mentally has an enormous advantage during crisis response.

Detective 369 reveals how crisis-prepared executives create emergency Memory Palaces that contain all information needed for rapid decision-making. These aren't comprehensive databases, but carefully curated collections of critical information that could be needed during emergency situations. The emergency Memory Palace includes contact information for key personnel, regulatory requirements for crisis communication, financial reserves and insurance coverage, and strategic options for different crisis scenarios.

The contact information component uses alphabetical organization for rapid access during emergency communications. Key personnel are organized by function rather than hierarchy, ensuring that the right expertise can be reached immediately. Regulatory contacts, legal counsel, public relations support, and financial advisors all receive dedicated storage that makes them instantly accessible when needed.

Financial information receives Major System treatment that makes critical numbers immediately available during crisis decision-making. Insurance coverage limits, credit line availability, cash reserves, and regulatory filing requirements become memorable images that can be recalled under pressure. This financial awareness allows leaders to make informed decisions about crisis response strategies without waiting for detailed financial analysis.

The strategic options component uses linking techniques that connect different crisis scenarios to appropriate response strategies. Product recall procedures, regulatory violation responses, competitive attack counters, and operational failure protocols become narrative sequences that can be accessed quickly when specific crisis types emerge. These pre-planned response frameworks ensure that crisis decisions are informed by comprehensive strategic thinking rather than panic reactions.

Detective 369 emphasizes that crisis memory systems must be maintained and updated regularly to remain effective. Crisis scenarios evolve, personnel changes occur, and regulatory requirements shift over time. Effective crisis leaders use spaced repetition techniques to keep their emergency Memory Palaces current and accessible. This ongoing maintenance ensures that crisis response capabilities remain sharp even during peaceful periods.

The communication component requires specialized memory techniques for delivering clear, accurate information under extreme pressure. Crisis communications must be precise, consistent, and carefully coordinated across multiple stakeholders. The leader who can remember key messages, factual details, and communication protocols without consulting notes maintains credibility during the most challenging moments.

The Field Assignment: Your Corporate Intelligence Mission

Detective 369 closes his briefcase and turns to face you directly. This isn't just theoretical training–it's a practical mission that will test your ability to apply memory techniques in real business situations. Your assignment is to create and deploy a comprehensive Business Memory System that gives you a measurable competitive advantage in your professional environment.

Your mission consists of three operational phases, each designed to build different aspects of business memory mastery. Success at each phase will demonstrate your ability to transform memory techniques from academic exercises into practical business tools that enhance your professional effectiveness.

Phase One: Corporate Intelligence Gathering

Your first challenge is to create a comprehensive Business Memory Palace that organizes all the professional information you need to perform at your highest level. This includes client information, financial data, competitive intelligence, and strategic knowledge that drives success in your specific business environment.

Begin by selecting a familiar business location–your office building, a conference center you frequent, or a business complex you know well. Conduct a mental reconnaissance of this location, identifying specific areas where different types of professional information can be systematically stored. Map out designated zones for client data, financial information, competitive intelligence, and strategic knowledge.

Populate your Business Memory Palace with the most critical information you need to master. Client contact details, conversation history, and relationship dynamics should receive prime storage locations. Financial figures, budget allocations, and performance metrics need systematic organization using Major System techniques. Competitive intelligence and market information require linking approaches that connect related pieces of information through logical narratives.

Test your system by accessing information randomly throughout your business day. Can you recall client preferences without consulting notes? Can you cite financial figures during meetings without referencing reports? Can you discuss competitive positioning without preparation? The goal is to demonstrate that your Business Memory Palace provides faster, more reliable access to professional information than traditional external memory aids.

Phase Two: Relationship Intelligence Network

Your second challenge involves creating a comprehensive system for managing business relationships that gives you a significant advantage in networking, sales, and partnership development. This system must handle contact information, conversation history, personal preferences, and relationship development opportunities across all your professional connections.

Apply Memory Palace techniques to organize relationship information using locations that reflect the context where these relationships matter most. Conference centers, industry events, client offices, or networking venues can serve as the foundation for relationship Memory Palaces. Within these locations, create dedicated storage areas for different types of relationship information.

Use association techniques to connect names with faces, companies with industries, and personal details with professional opportunities. Each business contact should become a memorable character with distinctive characteristics that make them impossible to forget. Practice accessing relationship information quickly enough to support natural conversation flow during business interactions.

Implement follow-up systems that leverage your relationship memory to create personalized communications that reference specific conversation details and demonstrate genuine interest in your contacts' business challenges. Track the effectiveness of your relationship memory system by measuring improvements in networking outcomes, client relationships, and business development opportunities.

Phase Three: Executive Presence Integration

Your final challenge involves integrating all your business memory techniques into a comprehensive system that supports executive-level performance across all professional situations. This includes presentation delivery, meeting leadership, crisis management, and strategic decision-making capabilities that demonstrate mastery-level business memory.

Prepare and deliver a significant business presentation using only Memory Palace techniques for content organization. The presentation should be substantive enough to demonstrate your ability to handle complex material without external support. Practice adapting your content dynamically based on audience reactions and questions.

Apply your memory systems during high-stakes business situations where memory lapses could have professional consequences. This might include important client meetings, strategic planning sessions, budget reviews, or competitive presentations. Document the advantages your memory mastery provides compared to colleagues who rely on external memory aids.

Develop crisis management capabilities by creating emergency Memory Palaces that contain critical information for rapid decision-making under pressure. Test these systems through scenario planning exercises that simulate high-stress business situations requiring immediate access to complex information.

The Master Detective's Revelation: Why Memory Conquers Markets

Detective 369 walks to the floor-to-ceiling windows overlooking the city's financial district, where thousands of professionals compete daily for market share, client relationships, and career advancement. The ultimate secret of business success, he reflects, isn't superior intelligence, better technology, or more resources–it's the ability to access and apply information more effectively than your competitors.

In the information economy, memory has become the ultimate competitive weapon. While others fumble with devices, consult notes, or pause conversations to verify details, the executive with perfect recall maintains continuous engagement and authority. This isn't just about impressing clients–it's about building the kind of comprehensive situational awareness that enables superior decision-making and strategic thinking.

Detective 369 has observed that memory mastery creates a cascade of professional advantages that compound over time. Better information recall leads to more informed decisions. More informed decisions generate better business outcomes. Better business outcomes create enhanced credibility and reputation. Enhanced credibility opens doors to bigger opportunities and higher-level responsibilities. The executive who invests in memory mastery isn't just improving their recall–they're accelerating their entire career trajectory.

The competitive advantages extend beyond individual performance to organizational effectiveness. Teams led by executives with superior memory perform better because information flows more efficiently, decisions are made more quickly, and strategic coordination is enhanced. The organization becomes more agile, more responsive, and more capable of executing complex initiatives successfully.

Perhaps most importantly, memory mastery creates a sense of professional confidence that influences every business interaction. The executive who knows they can access any needed information instantly approaches meetings, presentations, and negotiations with a level of self-assurance that competitors find difficult to match. This confidence becomes a self-fulfilling prophecy that generates the very success it projects.

The Investigation Continues: Building Your Business Empire

Detective 369 turns from the window and walks toward the elevator, his investigation of business memory complete but his work far from finished. The techniques he's revealed aren't just memory aids–they're business tools that can transform your professional effectiveness and accelerate your career development in ways that traditional business education cannot match.

The key to long-term success with business memory techniques is understanding that they must be systematically developed and continuously maintained. Detective 369 has been refining his corporate memory systems for decades, adapting them to new business challenges and expanding them to accommodate growing professional responsibilities. Your business memory system should evolve with your career, becoming more sophisticated as your role and responsibilities expand.

Remember that business memory mastery is ultimately about creating professional freedom. Freedom from dependence on external memory aids, freedom from the anxiety of forgotten details, and freedom to engage fully in every business situation with complete confidence in your preparation and knowledge. These techniques don't just make you a better performer–they make you a more valuable leader, colleague, and business partner.

The investment in memory mastery pays dividends that compound throughout your career. The relationships you build through superior recall, the decisions you make with comprehensive information access, and the reputation you develop for preparation and competence create opportunities that would otherwise remain hidden. In the competitive landscape of modern business, memory isn't just an advantage–it's a necessity.

Detective 369 steps into the elevator as the doors slide shut with a quiet whisper. The fog of information overload that clouds so many business careers begin to clear when you master these memory techniques. Random data becomes organized intelligence, overwhelming information becomes systematic knowledge, and the chaos of modern business becomes a navigable landscape where memory provides the ultimate competitive advantage.

The corporate world awaits, and now you have the intelligence tools to dominate it.

Chapter 11: Advanced Learning Strategies

Detective 369 stands in the state-of-the-art forensic laboratory, surrounded by gleaming instruments and cutting-edge technology that would have been pure science fiction when he first began his career. Digital microscopes, DNA sequencers, spectrometers, and chemical analysis equipment fill the space like a modern detective's arsenal. But tonight, he's not here to analyze evidence–he's here to master the art of mastering itself. After decades of investigation, he's discovered that the most powerful skill a detective can possess isn't the ability to solve individual cases, but the ability to continuously learn, adapt, and build interconnected knowledge networks that make every new skill easier to acquire.

The modern investigative landscape changes with breathtaking speed. New forensic techniques emerge monthly, criminal methods evolve constantly, and the sheer volume of information that a detective must master grows exponentially each year. Traditional learning approaches–reading textbooks, attending lectures, and hoping knowledge sticks–simply can't keep pace with the demands of continuous professional development.

Detective 369 has spent the last phase of his career investigating a different kind of mystery: how expert learners acquire new skills with remarkable efficiency while others struggle to master even basic concepts. What he's discovered has transformed not just his own learning capabilities, but his entire approach to building expertise. The secret isn't working harder or studying longer–it's building interconnected knowledge networks that make new information naturally integrate with existing skills.

Tonight, Detective 369 reveals the advanced learning strategies that separate lifelong learners from those who plateau early in their careers. These aren't just memory techniques–they're systematic approaches to skill acquisition that accelerate expertise development across any domain.

The Knowledge Network: Understanding How Experts Think

Detective 369 walks to a wall covered with an intricate web of connections–strings linking photographs, documents, and evidence markers in a complex pattern that would appear chaotic to the untrained eye. This is his visual representation of how expert knowledge works: not as isolated facts stored in separate mental filing cabinets, but as interconnected networks where each piece of information strengthens and illuminates countless others.

The traditional model of learning, Detective 369 explains, treats knowledge like a library where books are organized by subject and stored separately on different shelves. Students learn about chemistry in one class, biology in another, and physics in a third, with little understanding of how these domains connect and reinforce each other. This compartmentalized approach might work for basic education, but it fails completely when dealing with the complex, interdisciplinary challenges that define expert performance.

Expert knowledge, by contrast, functions like Detective 369's evidence wall—a dynamic network where every piece of information is connected to multiple others through various types of relationships. When a forensic expert analyzes a blood sample, they're not just applying chemistry knowledge in isolation. They're simultaneously drawing on their understanding of human physiology, crime scene dynamics, evidence preservation protocols, legal requirements, and statistical analysis. Each domain of knowledge informs and strengthens the others, creating a robust web of expertise that can handle novel situations with remarkable flexibility.

Detective 369 has discovered that this network structure isn't just a byproduct of expertise—it's the foundation upon which all advanced learning is built. The experts who can quickly master new skills aren't necessarily more intelligent or naturally gifted. They're simply better at recognizing patterns, making connections, and integrating new information into existing knowledge networks. They've learned to learn systemically rather than in isolation.

This insight has profound implications for how Detective 369 approaches mastering new forensic techniques. Instead of studying each new method as a separate skill, he focuses on understanding how it connects to his existing knowledge base. When learning about new DNA analysis techniques, he doesn't just memorize procedures—he maps the connections between molecular biology, statistical analysis, evidence handling, and legal testimony. This interconnected approach allows him to master new techniques faster and apply them more effectively in real-world situations.

The Integration Protocol: Building Cross-Domain Connections

Detective 369 moves to his desk and opens a specialized notebook that looks unlike any traditional study guide. Instead of linear notes organized by subject, the pages contain diagrams, flowcharts, and concept maps that show how different domains of knowledge interconnect. This is his Integration Protocol–a systematic approach to building the cross-domain connections that characterize expert knowledge.

1. Pattern Recognition Across Domains: When learning any new skill or technique, he doesn't just focus on the specific procedures—he identifies the underlying patterns that connect the new information to his existing knowledge base. These patterns might be structural (similar processes or sequences), functional (similar purposes or outcomes), or conceptual (similar theoretical frameworks).

When Detective 369 first encountered digital forensics, he could have approached it as an entirely new field requiring separate study. Instead, he recognized that many of the fundamental patterns were identical to traditional crime scene investigation. Both involve evidence preservation, chain of custody procedures, systematic analysis, and logical reasoning. The tools and techniques were different, but the underlying investigative patterns were remarkably similar. By focusing on these connections rather than the differences, he was able to master digital forensics techniques in a fraction of the time that might have been required for someone without his investigative background.

2. Analogical Mapping: This is the systematic process of identifying how new concepts relate to familiar ones through analogy and metaphor. Detective 369 has learned that the human brain naturally understands new information by comparing it to existing knowledge. Rather than fighting this tendency, expert learners harness it by consciously creating analogies that illuminate the connections between new and familiar concepts.

When studying advanced ballistics analysis, Detective 369 didn't just memorize formulas and procedures. He recognized that projectile motion follows many of the same principles as other dynamic systems he already understood. The trajectory of a bullet resembles the path of a thrown object, influenced by gravity, air resistance, and initial velocity. The energy transfer during impact follows conservation principles like those governing automobile collisions. By mapping these analogies systematically, he was able to understand complex ballistics concepts through the lens of familiar physics principles.

3. Contextual Bridging: This is the process of understanding how new skills apply across different contexts and situations. Expert learners don't just master techniques in isolation; they understand how those techniques adapt to different environments, constraints, and objectives. This contextual understanding is what allows experts to apply their knowledge flexibly and creatively when faced with novel situations.

Detective 369 demonstrates this principle through his mastery of interview techniques. The basic principles of effective interviewing–building rapport, asking open-ended questions, listening actively, and reading nonverbal cues–remain constant across different contexts. But the specific application of these principles varies dramatically depending on whether he's questioning a cooperative witness, a hostile suspect, or a traumatized victim. By understanding how the same fundamental techniques adapt to different contexts, he can apply his interviewing skills effectively in any situation.

The Skill Scaffolding System: Building Expertise Systematically

Detective 369 leads you to a training area where he's set up a progression of increasingly complex scenarios. This is his Skill Scaffolding System–a systematic approach to building expertise that ensures each new skill builds logically upon previously mastered foundations. The system is based on the principle that complex skills aren't learned all at once but are constructed through careful layering of simpler component skills.

1. Skill Decomposition: This is the process of breaking complex abilities into their component parts and understanding how those parts work together. Detective 369 has learned that most people struggle with new skills because they try to master everything simultaneously rather than building systematically from simple to complex. Expert learners, by contrast, identify the fundamental building blocks and master them sequentially.

When Detective 369 decided to master crime scene photography, he didn't start by trying to capture perfect images of complex scenes. Instead, he decomposed the skill into its component parts: understanding lighting principles, mastering camera settings, learning composition techniques, developing an eye for relevant details, and understanding how photographs would be used in legal proceedings. He then practiced each component separately before integrating them into comprehensive crime scene documentation skills.

The decomposition process requires understanding not just what the components are, but how they interact with each other. Detective 369 recognized that crime scene photography wasn't just about technical camera skills–it required understanding evidence preservation, legal requirements, investigative priorities, and visual communication principles. Each component skill informed and strengthened the others, creating a robust foundation for expert performance.

2. Progressive Complexity: This is the systematic increase in difficulty that ensures each new challenge builds upon previously mastered skills. Detective 369 has observed that many people plateau in their learning because they either stay in their comfort zone too long or jump to challenges that exceed their current capability. Expert learners navigate this balance by carefully calibrating the difficulty of their practice to maintain optimal challenge levels.

Detective 369's approach to mastering interrogation techniques illustrates this principle perfectly. He began by practicing active listening skills in low-stakes conversations, then moved to structured interviews with cooperative witnesses, gradually progressing to more challenging situations with reluctant subjects, and finally to high-pressure interrogations with hostile suspects. Each level built upon the skills developed in previous stages while introducing new challenges that stretched his capabilities without overwhelming them.

The progression isn't just about increasing difficulty–it's about ensuring that each new level reinforces and strengthens the skills from previous levels. When Detective 369 practices advanced interrogation techniques, he's not just learning new methods; he's deepening his understanding of fundamental communication principles, sharpening his ability to read nonverbal cues, and refining his capacity to adapt his approach based on real-time feedback.

The Cross-Pollination Method: Transferring Skills Between Domains

Detective 369 opens a case file that contains an unusual collection of materials: medical journals, psychology research papers, military training manuals, and business strategy guides. This eclectic mix represents his Cross-Pollination Method–the systematic practice of identifying how insights from one domain can enhance performance in another. The method is based on the recognition that breakthrough innovations often occur at the intersection of different fields rather than within the boundaries of a single discipline.

1. Principle Extraction: This is the ability to identify fundamental principles that operate across different domains and contexts. Detective 369 has learned that while the surface features of different fields may appear unrelated, many of the underlying principles are remarkably similar. By focusing on these deeper patterns, he can transfer insights from one domain to another with remarkable effectiveness.

Detective 369's study of military tactics has profoundly influenced his approach to crime scene investigation. Both domains involve strategic thinking, resource allocation, risk assessment, and systematic planning. The military principle of "terrain analysis"–understanding how physical environment affects strategic options–translates directly to crime scene work, where the layout of spaces, available entry and exit points, and sight lines all influence how crimes unfold and how investigations should proceed.

The military concept of *"force multiplication"*–using tools and techniques to amplify human capabilities–has revolutionized Detective 369's approach to evidence analysis. Just as military units use technology and coordination to achieve objectives that would be impossible for individuals, investigative teams can use specialized tools, systematic procedures, and coordinated efforts to solve cases that would overwhelm any single detective.

2. Metaphorical Thinking: This is the systematic use of metaphors and analogies to understand new concepts through familiar frameworks. Detective 369 has discovered that metaphors aren't just literary devices; they're powerful cognitive tools that can illuminate hidden connections and suggest new approaches to complex problems.

Detective 369's understanding of criminal psychology has been enhanced by his study of medical diagnosis. Both doctors and detectives must gather symptoms or clues, generate hypotheses about underlying causes, test those hypotheses through further investigation, and arrive at conclusions that guide effective intervention. The medical concept of *"differential diagnosis"*–systematically ruling out alternative explanations–has become a cornerstone of Detective 369's investigative methodology.

The medical principle of *"vital signs"*–monitoring key indicators that reveal underlying health status–has transformed how Detective 369 approaches crime scene analysis. Just as doctors look for specific physiological indicators that suggest particular conditions, Detective 369 has learned to identify behavioral, physical, and circumstantial "vital signs" that suggest specific criminal patterns or motivations.

3. Adaptive Application: This is the ability to modify insights from one domain to fit the unique requirements of another. Detective 369 has learned that successful cross-pollination requires more than just identifying similarities; it requires understanding how principles must be adapted to work effectively in new contexts.

Detective 369's study of negotiation techniques from business and diplomacy has enhanced his suspect interrogation skills, but not through direct application. Business negotiation assumes that both parties have legitimate interests, and that win-win solutions are possible. Criminal interrogation, by contrast, often involves fundamental conflicts of interest where one party is actively trying to deceive the other. The principles of rapport-building, strategic concession-making, and psychological leverage apply to both domains, but they must be adapted to account for the different ethical frameworks and power dynamics involved.

The Rapid Mastery Framework: Accelerating Skill Acquisition

Detective 369 moves to a whiteboard covered with timelines, learning curves, and performance metrics. This is his Rapid Mastery Framework–a systematic approach to accelerating the acquisition of new skills without sacrificing depth or quality. The framework is based on years of research into how expert learners achieve mastery faster than their peers, and it represents the culmination of Detective 369's investigation into the science of skill acquisition.

1. Strategic Focus: This is the ability to identify and concentrate on the 20%

of skills that will generate 80% of the performance improvement. Detective 369 has observed that most people approach new skills by trying to learn everything at once, which dilutes their efforts and slows their progress. Expert learners, by contrast, identify the high-impact elements that will generate the greatest return on their learning investment.

When Detective 369 decided to master digital evidence analysis, he didn't try to become an expert in every software tool and technique simultaneously. Instead, he identified the core skills that would provide the foundation for all other learning: understanding file systems, recognizing digital artifacts, maintaining chain of custody, and documenting findings in legally admissible formats. By mastering these fundamental skills first, he created a platform that made all subsequent learning faster and more effective.

The strategic focus approach requires understanding not just what to learn, but what to ignore—at least initially. Detective 369 has learned that trying to master everything simultaneously leads to superficial understanding and poor retention. By focusing intensively on core skills until they become automatic, he creates cognitive space for more advanced techniques and specialized applications.

2. Deliberate Practice: This is the systematic approach to skill development that focuses on continuous improvement rather than mere repetition. Detective 369 has discovered that the quality of practice matters far more than the quantity. Experts don't just practice more; they practice differently, with focused attention on specific weaknesses and systematic efforts to push beyond their comfort zones.

Detective 369's approach to improving his deductive reasoning skills illustrates the principles of deliberate practice. Rather than simply reviewing old cases or reading about logical fallacies, he creates systematic exercises that challenge specific aspects of his reasoning abilities. He might practice generating alternative hypotheses for ambiguous evidence, identifying unstated assumptions in witness statements, or recognizing when his own biases might be influencing his conclusions.

Each practice session is designed with specific objectives, immediate feedback mechanisms, and measures of improvement. Detective 369 doesn't just practice until he gets something right once; he practices until he can perform consistently under pressure, with distractions, and in novel situations. This approach ensures that his skills remain sharp and reliable even in the most challenging circumstances.

3. Accelerated Feedback: This is the systematic gathering and use of performance information to guide skill development. Detective 369 has learned that feedback isn't just helpful for learning; it's essential. Without accurate, timely feedback, even the most dedicated practice can reinforce errors and build ineffective habits.

Detective 369 has developed sophisticated systems for gathering feedback on his performance across different skill domains. For interrogation skills, he might record practice sessions and analyze his questioning techniques, listening patterns, and response strategies. For evidence analysis, he might seek expert review of his conclusions and methodologies. For crime scene investigation, he might compare his initial assessments with the final case outcomes to identify areas for improvement.

The feedback systems aren't just about identifying mistakes; they're about understanding the underlying patterns that lead to both success and failure. Detective 369 has learned to treat each piece of feedback as data in an ongoing investigation into his own performance, systematically identifying the factors that contribute to his most effective work.

The Mastery Maintenance System: Preserving and Enhancing Expertise

Detective 369 walks to a wall chart that tracks his performance across dozens of different skills over several years. The chart reveals a fascinating pattern: some skills show steady improvement over time, others plateau at high levels, and a few decline without regular maintenance. This is his Mastery Maintenance System–a systematic approach to preserving and enhancing expertise over time.

1. Skill Inventory: This is the regular assessment of competencies across all domains of expertise. Detective 369 has learned that expertise isn't static; it requires continuous attention and deliberate effort to maintain peak performance. Without systematic maintenance, even well-developed skills can deteriorate over time, especially those that aren't used regularly.

Detective 369 conducts quarterly assessments of his skill inventory, evaluating his performance across all major areas of expertise. Some skills, like basic interview techniques, remain consistently strong because he uses them daily. Others, like specialized forensic procedures, require periodic refresher training to maintain proficiency. A few, like certain types of evidence analysis, might need intensive re-training if he hasn't used them for extended periods.

The inventory process isn't just about identifying weaknesses; it's about understanding how different skills interact and influence each other. Detective 369 has discovered that maintaining expertise in one area often supports performance in related areas. His ongoing development of psychological assessment skills enhances his interrogation abilities, while his study of new forensic techniques improves his general analytical thinking.

2. Continuous Challenge: This is the systematic introduction of new difficulties and complexities that prevent stagnation and promote continued growth. Detective 369 has observed that many professionals plateau in their development because they become too comfortable with familiar challenges. Expert learners, by contrast, actively seek out new difficulties that stretch their capabilities and force continued adaptation.

Detective 369 regularly takes on cases that push the boundaries of his expertise, volunteers for training programs that introduce new methodologies, and collaborates with experts from other fields who can provide fresh perspectives on familiar problems. These challenges aren't just about learning new techniques; they're about maintaining the cognitive flexibility and adaptability that characterize expert performance.

The challenge system includes both internal and external sources of difficulty. Internally, Detective 369 might impose additional constraints on familiar tasks, such as solving cases with limited information or working under compressed time frames. Externally, he might seek out complex cases that require integration of multiple skill domains or collaboration with unfamiliar expert communities.

3. Knowledge Network Expansion: This is the systematic addition of new connections and relationships within existing areas of expertise. Detective 369 has learned that expertise isn't just about knowing more facts; it's about understanding more connections between facts. The most profound improvements in expert performance often come from discovering new relationships between previously separate pieces of knowledge.

Detective 369 regularly engages in what he calls "connection mapping"–the systematic exploration of how different aspects of his expertise relate to each other. This might involve studying how psychological principles apply to evidence analysis, how technological advances affect investigative procedures, or how changes in legal standards influence case preparation strategies.

These connection mapping exercises often reveal unexpected insights that improve performance across multiple domains. Detective 369's study of how cognitive biases affect witness testimony has enhanced not just his interviewing skills, but also his evidence evaluation procedures, his case presentation techniques, and his approach to training other investigators.

The Field Assignment: Your Advanced Learning Investigation

Detective 369 closes his training materials and turns to face you with the intense focus of someone about to assign a mission that will test everything you've learned. This isn't just practice–it's a comprehensive investigation into your own learning capabilities that will demonstrate whether you can apply advanced learning strategies to real-world skill development.

Your mission, should you choose to accept it, is to identify a complex skill relevant to your professional or personal development and apply Detective 369's advanced learning strategies to accelerate your mastery. This skill should be substantial enough to require genuine effort and sophisticated enough to benefit from interconnected knowledge networks.

The investigation consists of three phases, each designed to test different aspects of advanced learning strategy implementation. Success at each phase will demonstrate your ability to think like an expert learner and build the kind of knowledge networks that separate masters from amateurs.

Phase One: Network Mapping and Skill Decomposition

Your first challenge is to conduct a comprehensive analysis of your chosen skill using Detective 369's Integration Protocol. Begin by mapping the knowledge networks that surround your target skill. Identify at least five different domains of knowledge that connect to your chosen skill and analyze how each domain contributes to expert performance.

Create a visual representation of these connections, showing how different aspects of knowledge interact and reinforce each other. This might be a concept map, a flowchart, or any other format that clearly illustrates the relationships between different domains of expertise.

Next, apply the Skill Scaffolding System to decompose your chosen skill into its component parts. Identify the fundamental building blocks that must be mastered before more advanced techniques can be learned effectively. Arrange these components in a logical sequence that builds from simple to complex, ensuring that each level provides a solid foundation for the next.

Document your analysis in a comprehensive report that demonstrates your understanding of how expert knowledge is structured and how complex skills can be learned systematically. The report should show clear evidence of pattern recognition, analogical thinking, and strategic focus.

Phase Two: Cross-Domain Application and Rapid Mastery

Your second challenge involves applying Detective 369's Cross-Pollination Method to accelerate your skill development. Identify at least three different fields or domains that might provide insights relevant to your chosen skill. These should be areas that initially seem unrelated but share underlying principles or patterns.

For each domain, extract specific principles, techniques, or insights that could enhance your performance in your target skill. Create detailed analogies that explain how these cross-domain insights apply to your learning objectives. Test these applications through deliberate practice, documenting both successes and failures.

Implement Detective 369's Rapid Mastery Framework by identifying the 20% of skills that will generate 80% of your performance improvement. Focus your practice efforts on these high-impact elements, using deliberate practice techniques to ensure rapid but thorough development.

Create a feedback system that provides regular, specific information about your performance. This might involve recording practice sessions, seek expert evaluation, or designing objective measures of improvement. Use this feedback to guide your practice and identify areas needing additional attention.

Phase Three: Integration and Mastery Maintenance

Your final challenge is to demonstrate that you can integrate your newly developed skills into your broader expertise and create systems for long-term maintenance. Show how your target skill connects to your existing knowledge base and enhances your overall competence.

Develop a comprehensive Mastery Maintenance System that will preserve and enhance your new skills over time. This should include regular assessment procedures, continuous challenge mechanisms, and strategies for expanding your knowledge networks.

Create a detailed plan for how you will continue developing this skill over the next year, including specific milestones, practice schedules, and evaluation criteria. The plan should demonstrate your understanding of how expertise develops over time and how to maintain peak performance.

Document your entire learning journey in a comprehensive case report that could serve as a model for others attempting to master similar skills. The report should demonstrate not just what you learned, but how you learned it and why your approach was effective.

The Master Detective's Revelation: The Art of Learning to Learn

Detective 369 stands at his window, looking out at the city lights that sparkle like neural connections in the vast network of human knowledge. The advanced learning strategies he's revealed tonight aren't just techniques for acquiring new skills–they're tools for transforming how you think about learning itself. Master these approaches, and you don't just become better at memorizing information; you become better at understanding how expertise develops and how to accelerate your own professional growth.

The research is clear and compelling: expert learners don't just know more than novices; they think differently about knowledge itself. They see connections where others see isolation, recognize patterns where others see randomness, and understand systems where others see only components. These cognitive differences aren't innate talents–they're learnable skills that can be developed through systematic practice and strategic application.

Detective 369 has discovered that the most profound learning occurs not when you master individual techniques, but when you understand the principles underlying all effective learning. When you can recognize how knowledge networks develop, how skills transfer between domains, and how expertise is maintained over time, you develop what researchers call "learning how to learn"–the meta-skill that makes all other learning faster and more effective.

The advanced learning strategies aren't just about professional development; they're about intellectual freedom. Freedom from the anxiety of information overload, freedom from the limitations of traditional educational approaches, and freedom to explore new domains of knowledge with confidence and systematic effectiveness. These techniques don't just make you a better learner– they make you a more capable, adaptable, and intellectually confident person.

Perhaps most importantly, these strategies create a sense of mastery over your own cognitive development. Instead of feeling overwhelmed by the pace of change in your field, you develop systematic approaches for staying current and continuously improving. Instead of being limited by your formal education, you create frameworks for lifelong learning that adapt to your changing needs and interests.

The Investigation Continues: Building Your Learning Empire

Detective 369 turns from the window and walks toward the door, his investigation of advanced learning strategies complete but his work far from finished. The techniques he's revealed represent the culmination of decades of research into how expert learners develop and maintain their capabilities. They're not just memory tricks or study techniques–they're systematic approaches to cognitive development that can transform how you approach any learning challenge.

The key to long-term success with these strategies is understanding that they must be developed systematically and applied consistently. Detective 369 has been refining his approach to learning for decades, and he's still discovering new applications and improvements. Your learning system should evolve with your needs, becoming more sophisticated as your expertise develops and your challenges become more complex.

Remember that advanced learning is ultimately about creating intellectual leverage. By understanding how knowledge networks develop, how skills transfer between domains, and how expertise is maintained over time, you can achieve levels of performance that would be impossible through traditional approaches. These techniques don't just help you learn faster–they help you think more clearly, solve problems more effectively, and adapt more readily to changing circumstances.

The investment in advanced learning strategies pays dividends that compound throughout your career. The knowledge networks you build, the connections you discover, and the skills you develop create opportunities that would otherwise remain hidden. In an era of rapid change and increasing complexity, the ability to learn continuously and effectively isn't just an advantage–it's a necessity.

Detective 369 pauses at the threshold, his hand on the brass doorknob. The fog of information overload that clouds so many professional careers begin to clear when you master these advanced learning strategies. Random facts become organized knowledge, overwhelming complexity becomes manageable challenge, and the chaos of continuous change becomes a navigable landscape where learning provides the ultimate competitive advantage.

The modern world demands lifelong learners, and now you have the tools to meet that demand with confidence and systematic effectiveness.

Chapter 12: Building Your Personal Memory System

Detective 369 stands in his private study, surrounded by the accumulated wisdom of decades of investigation. The walls are lined with case files, evidence boards, and reference materials–but these aren't the tools that make him legendary. The real power lies in the invisible arsenal he's built inside his mind: a comprehensive memory system that can adapt to any challenge, store any information, and retrieve any detail with precision. Tonight, in this final chapter, he's going to help you build your own Master Detective's Toolkit–a personalized memory system that will serve you for a lifetime.

After eleven chapters of investigation, you've learned the individual techniques that transform ordinary minds into extraordinary ones. You've mastered the art of association, discovered the power of spatial memory, and wielded the precision of numerical systems. But knowing these techniques in isolation is like having a collection of fine instruments scattered across a workbench. The true mastery comes from assembling them into a unified system–your personal memory arsenal that can handle any intellectual challenge you'll face.

Detective 369 has spent his career not just learning memory techniques, but perfecting the art of combining them into seamless, powerful systems. He knows that the difference between a skilled amateur and a true master isn't the number of techniques you know–it's how elegantly you integrate them into a personal approach that matches your unique mind, your specific needs, and your individual goals.

Tonight, he reveals the blueprint for constructing your own Master Detective's Toolkit, a comprehensive memory system that will grow with you throughout your life and adapt to whatever challenges await in your future investigations.

The Foundation: Assessing Your Memory Landscape

Detective 369 walks to his desk and opens a thick portfolio labeled "Personal Memory Assessment." Inside are detailed analyses of different memory profiles, learning styles, and cognitive preferences that he's observed over decades of training fellow investigators. The first step in building your personal memory system, he explains, isn't learning new techniques–it's understanding the unique landscape of your own mind.

Every detective has natural strengths and areas that require more systematic development. Some investigators naturally excel at spatial reasoning, making Memory Palace techniques feel intuitive from the first attempt. Others have powerful associative thinking that makes linking methods and substitution techniques flow effortlessly. Still others possess exceptional attention to detail that makes numerical systems and precise recall their strongest assets.

Detective 369 has developed a systematic approach to memory assessment that reveals your natural cognitive preferences. The process begins with honest self-reflection about your current memory experiences. When you naturally remember something well, what type of information is it? Visual details like faces and scenes? Spatial relationships like routes and locations? Sequential patterns like stories and procedures? Numerical data like dates and statistics? Understanding your natural memory strengths provides the foundation upon which you'll build your personalized system.

The assessment continues with deliberate experimentation across different memory domains. Detective 369 recommends spending a week focusing intensively on visual memory techniques, paying attention to how easily you can create vivid mental images and how well those images persist over time. The following week, concentrate on spatial memory approaches, testing your ability to navigate Memory Palaces and organize information by location. Continue this systematic exploration through sequential memory, associative thinking, and numerical encoding.

This experimental phase reveals not just what you're naturally good at, but what feels engaging and sustainable for long-term practice. Detective 369 emphasizes that the most sophisticated memory system in the world is useless if you don't enjoy using it. Your personal memory toolkit must feel natural, engaging, and personally meaningful, or it will gradually fall into disuse despite its theoretical power.

The assessment also identifies your specific information challenges–the types of memory tasks that are most important in your professional and personal life. A medical student faces different memory demands than a business executive, a language learner, or a history enthusiast. Your personal memory system should be optimized for the information you need to master, not for abstract demonstration of memory techniques.

Detective 369 has observed that the most successful memory practitioners are those who begin with their strongest natural abilities and gradually expand into other domains. This approach builds confidence and momentum while ensuring that your memory system remains practical and immediately useful. You don't need to be equally skilled in all techniques–you need to be exceptionally skilled in the approaches that matter most for your specific goals.

The Architecture: Designing Your Core Memory Infrastructure

Detective 369 leads you to his evidence room, where different organizational systems work together in perfect harmony. Memory Palaces house complex spatial information, numerical peg systems organize sequential data, and associative networks connect related concepts across different domains. This isn't chaos–it's carefully designed architecture where each system serves a specific purpose while contributing to a unified whole.

Building your personal memory infrastructure requires understanding how different techniques can work together synergistically rather than in isolation. Detective 369 has discovered that the most powerful memory systems aren't built by mastering individual techniques, but by creating elegant integrations where each method enhances the others.

The foundation of your memory architecture should be built around your strongest natural abilities. If spatial memory is your strength, your core system might center on multiple Memory Palaces, each dedicated to different types of information. Your childhood home might house personal memories and family information, your current workplace could organize professional knowledge, and familiar public spaces might contain academic or hobby-related learning. These spatial frameworks provide the structural backbone around which other techniques can be integrated.

For those with strong associative thinking, the core architecture might emphasize linking methods and substitution techniques, creating vast networks of connected information where each new piece of knowledge strengthens and illuminates existing understanding. The major organizational principle becomes thematic connection rather than spatial location, with information grouped by meaning, similarity, and logical relationship.

Detective 369 emphasizes that regardless of your core approach, a complete memory system requires integration across multiple domains. Even the most spatially oriented system benefits from numerical encoding for dates, statistics, and precise data. Even the most associative structured system gains power from spatial organization for complex, multi-faceted information.

The key to successful integration is creating clear protocols for how different techniques interact. Detective 369 has developed systematic approaches for moving information between different memory systems as needed. Spatial information from Memory Palaces can be converted to numerical codes for precise recall. Associative networks can be given spatial structure for better organization. Sequential information can be encoded both spatially and numerically for maximum reliability.

Your memory architecture should also include specialized sub-systems for different types of information challenges. Detective 369 maintains separate organizational approaches for temporary information that needs short-term retention, permanent knowledge that requires long-term accessibility, and dynamic information that changes regularly and needs systematic updating.

The infrastructure should be scalable, allowing you to expand capacity and add new organizational layers as your knowledge grows and your needs evolve. Detective 369's memory system has grown continuously throughout his career, adding new Memory Palaces, expanding numerical systems, and developing more sophisticated associative networks. Your system should be designed for growth rather than static completion.

The Integration Protocol: Combining Techniques for Maximum Power

Detective 369 opens a manual titled "Advanced Integration Techniques" and reveals the systematic approaches he's developed for combining different memory methods into unified, powerful systems. The true art of memory mastery, he explains, lies not in using techniques individually, but in orchestrating them together to create effects that exceed the sum of their parts.

The integration protocol begins with understanding the natural synergies between different memory techniques. The Memory Palace method provides excellent spatial organization but benefits from numerical encoding for precise positioning and sequential recall. The Major System creates powerful numerical associations but gains narrative flow when integrated with linking methods. The Alphabet PEG System offers systematic categorical organization but becomes more memorable when combined with vivid imagery and spatial placement.

Detective 369 demonstrates this principle through his approach to mastering complex professional knowledge. When learning about new forensic techniques, he doesn't just memorize procedures–he creates comprehensive information networks that connect spatial, numerical, and associative elements. The basic procedure gets encoded in a Memory Palace, providing step-by-step spatial organization. Key numerical data gets converted through the Major System, creating precise recall for measurements, timelines, and statistical information. Related concepts get linked through associative networks, ensuring that new techniques connect meaningfully to existing knowledge.

The integration process requires developing systematic protocols for information triage–determining which memory technique is most appropriate for each type of information you encounter. Detective 369 has created decision trees that guide this selection process automatically. Spatial information naturally goes to Memory Palaces, numerical data gets processed through the Major System, categorical information fits the Alphabet PEG System, and complex relationships get developed through associative linking.

But the most powerful integrations occur when single pieces of information get encoded through multiple techniques simultaneously. Detective 369's approach to remembering important names illustrates this multi-layered encoding. A new contact's name gets processed through phonetic substitution to create visual imagery, the visual image gets placed in a Memory Palace location that reflects the relationship context, and the person's professional details get organized through numerical or alphabetical systems as appropriate.

This redundant encoding creates multiple retrieval pathways for the same information, making forgetting virtually impossible. If one memory pathway becomes temporarily inaccessible, others provide alternative routes to the same information. The redundancy also strengthens the overall memory trace, making information more durable and resistant to interference.

Detective 369 emphasizes that successful integration requires practice and systematic development. You can't simply combine techniques arbitrarily–you need to develop fluency with each method individually before attempting sophisticated combinations. The integration skills build gradually through deliberate practice and systematic experimentation.

The Maintenance System: Keeping Your Memory Sharp

Detective 369 walks to a calendar covered with systematic review schedules, practice routines, and maintenance protocols. Building a powerful memory system is only the beginning, he explains. The real challenge lies in maintaining peak performance over time, ensuring that your mental tools remain sharp and accessible whenever you need them.

The maintenance system begins with regular practice routines that keep your fundamental memory skills operating at peak efficiency. Detective 369 has developed daily exercises that maintain his ability to create vivid mental imagery, navigate Memory Palaces smoothly, and convert numbers to images automatically. These aren't lengthy training sessions–they're brief, focused activities that can be integrated into normal daily routines.

The practice routines rotate through different memory domains to ensure comprehensive maintenance. Monday might focus on Memory Palace navigation, Tuesday on numerical conversion practice, Wednesday on associative linking exercises, Thursday on recall and retrieval drills, and Friday on integration challenges that combine multiple techniques. This systematic rotation prevents any single skill from deteriorating through neglect.

Detective 369 also emphasizes the importance of systematic review using spaced repetition principles. The information stored in your memory system doesn't maintain itself–it requires strategic review at optimal intervals to prevent forgetting. He's developed protocols for reviewing different types of information at different schedules, with personally important information getting more frequent review than secondary details.

The maintenance system includes regular assessment and adjustment procedures. Detective 369 conducts monthly evaluations of his memory system's effectiveness, identifying areas that need attention and techniques that might need refinement. He tracks which methods are working well, which are falling into disuse, and which need to be modified to better serve his evolving needs.

The system also accommodates the natural changes that occur in memory and cognition over time. Detective 369 has observed that memory capabilities don't remain static throughout life–they evolve, mature, and sometimes require adaptation to maintain peak performance. Your memory system should be flexible enough to accommodate these changes while maintaining its core effectiveness.

Most importantly, the maintenance system includes procedures for continuing to expand and develop your memory capabilities. Detective 369 has never stopped learning new techniques, refining existing methods, and discovering novel applications for familiar approaches. Your memory system should be designed for continuous growth rather than static maintenance.

The Specialization Modules: Customizing for Your Unique Needs

Detective 369 opens a series of specialized filing cabinets, each one designed for specific types of information challenges. While your core memory system provides general-purpose capability, he explains, true mastery requires developing specialized modules that address the unique demands of your professional and personal interests.

The specialization process begins with identifying the specific types of information that are most critical to your success and satisfaction. A medical professional needs specialized systems for anatomical knowledge, drug information, and diagnostic procedures. A business leader requires modules for financial data, strategic information, and relationship management. A student needs systems optimized for academic content, exam preparation, and research organization.

Detective 369 has developed specialized modules for different aspects of his investigative work. His witness interview module combines Memory Palace techniques with numerical encoding to create comprehensive records of conversations, including dialogue, nonverbal cues, and environmental context. His evidence analysis module integrates associative linking with spatial organization to track complex relationships between physical evidence, witness statements, and case theories.

Each specialization module represents a focused application of general memory principles to specific information domains. The modules aren't entirely separate systems–they're specialized applications of your core memory infrastructure, optimized for types of challenges while maintaining integration with your broader memory architecture.

The development of specialization modules requires deep understanding of both memory techniques and the specific information domain you're targeting. Detective 369 emphasizes that effective specialization comes from understanding not just how to use memory techniques, but how information in your field naturally organizes, what types of recall are most important, and what kinds of errors are most dangerous.

Professional specialization modules should address the specific recall challenges you face in your work environment. If you need to remember client information during meetings, your module should optimize for quick retrieval of personal details, conversation history, and relationship context. If you need to master technical procedures, your module should focus on sequential memory and error prevention. If you need to handle large volumes of numerical data, your module should emphasize systematic organization and cross-referencing capabilities.

Personal specialization modules can address your hobbies, interests, and lifelong learning goals. Detective 369 has developed modules for art history, wine appreciation, and classical music–areas of personal interest that enrich his life beyond his professional responsibilities. These modules use the same systematic approaches as his professional systems but are optimized for enjoyment and personal satisfaction rather than job performance.

The Evolution Path: Growing Your System Over Time

Detective 369 leads you to a timeline that charts the evolution of his memory system over several decades. What began as simple techniques for remembering names and faces has evolved into a comprehensive cognitive architecture that supports every aspect of his professional and personal life. Your memory system, he explains, should be designed not just for your current needs, but for the person you're becoming and the challenges you'll face in the future.

The evolution path begins with mastering foundational techniques thoroughly before adding complexity. Detective 369 started with basic Memory Palace construction and simple linking methods, practicing these core skills until they became automatic and effortless. Only after achieving fluency with the fundamentals **did he begin** adding numerical systems, advanced integration techniques, and specialized modules.

This foundation-first approach ensures that your memory system remains stable and reliable as it grows. Each new technique or capability builds upon solid existing skills rather than creating a fragile structure that might collapse under pressure. Detective 369 has observed that memory practitioners who try to implement too many techniques simultaneously often end up with systems that are theoretically sophisticated but practically unreliable.

The evolution process includes systematic expansion of capacity and capability. As your core techniques become more fluent, you can gradually add new Memory Palaces, expand numerical systems, and develop more sophisticated associative networks. Detective 369's system has grown from a single Memory Palace to a complex network of interconnected mental spaces, each serving specific functions while contributing to the unified whole.

The path also includes periodic renovation and optimization. Detective 369 regularly reviews his memory system to identify techniques that are no longer serving their intended purpose, information that needs to be reorganized, and methods that could be refined for better performance. This isn't just maintenance—**it's** active improvement based on experience and changing needs.

The evolution path should accommodate the natural changes that occur in your life circumstances, professional responsibilities, and personal interests. Detective 369's system has adapted to changes in investigative technology, shifts in legal procedures, and evolution in his own cognitive capabilities. Your system should be flexible enough to accommodate similar changes while maintaining its core effectiveness.

Most importantly, the evolution path includes mechanisms for discovering and integrating new memory techniques as they become available. Detective 369 continues to study new research in cognitive science, experiment with novel applications of familiar techniques, and learn from other memory practitioners. Your system should be designed for continuous learning and improvement rather than static completion.

The Field Assignment: Constructing Your Master Detective's Toolkit

Detective 369 closes his files and turns to face you with the intensity of someone about to assign the most important mission of your training. This isn't just another exercise–it's the comprehensive project that will transform you from a student of memory techniques into a master of your own cognitive capabilities.

Your mission is to design, build, and deploy a complete personal memory system that integrates everything you've learned into a unified toolkit perfectly suited to your unique needs, goals, and circumstances. This system should be comprehensive enough to handle any memory challenge you might face, yet elegant enough to use effortlessly in your daily life.

The project consists of four phases, each building upon the previous one to create a complete transformation of your memory capabilities. Success at each phase will demonstrate your mastery of not just individual techniques, but the higher-level skills of system design, integration, and optimization.

Phase One: Foundation Assessment and Core Design

Your first challenge is to conduct a comprehensive assessment of your current memory capabilities and design the core architecture for your personal system. Begin by systematically evaluating your natural memory strengths and weaknesses across different domains–spatial, visual, numerical, associative, and sequential. Use the assessment protocols Detective 369 has described, spending at least a week exploring each domain through focused practice and experimentation.

Document your findings in a detailed analysis that identifies your strongest natural abilities, your areas needing development, and the specific types of memory challenges that are most important in your professional and personal life. This analysis should provide the foundation for all subsequent design decisions.

Based on your assessment, design the core architecture for your personal memory system. Choose the primary organizational approach that best matches your natural strengths–whether spatial, associative, numerical, or some combination. Plan how different techniques will integrate within this architecture, creating clear protocols for information triage and systematic approaches for moving information between different memory systems.

Create a detailed blueprint for your system that includes your core Memory Palace designs, numerical encoding preferences, associative linking strategies, and integration protocols. This blueprint should be specific enough to guide implementation while flexible enough to accommodate future evolution and expansion.

Phase Two: Implementation and Integration

Your second challenge is to implement your designed system and develop fluency with its integrated operation. Begin by building your core Memory Palace infrastructure, creating the spatial frameworks that will house your most important information. Practice navigating these spaces until the movement feels natural and automatic, ensuring that your spatial architecture is solid and reliable.

Implement your numerical encoding systems, building the peg lists and conversion skills that will handle all quantitative information in your system. Practice until number-to-image conversion becomes automatic, creating the fluency necessary for real-time application during complex memory tasks.

Develop your associative linking networks, creating the connection strategies that will integrate new information with existing knowledge. Practice building these networks until associative thinking becomes a natural part of how you process and organize information.

Test your integration protocols by working with complex, multi-faceted information that requires multiple memory techniques working together. Practice moving information between different parts of your system until the integration feels seamless and natural.

Phase Three: Specialization and Optimization

Your third challenge is to develop specialized modules for your most important information domains and optimize your system for peak performance. Identify the specific types of information that are most critical to your professional success and personal satisfaction, then create specialized applications of your core memory system to address these needs.

Develop professional specialization modules that address the specific recall challenges you face in your work environment. These modules should integrate seamlessly with your core system while providing optimized approaches for your most important professional information.

Create personal specialization modules for your hobbies, interests, and lifelong learning goals. These modules should use the same systematic approaches as your professional systems but be optimized for enjoyment and personal satisfaction.

Optimize your system for peak performance by identifying and eliminating bottlenecks, streamlining frequently used procedures, and refining techniques based on real-world usage patterns. This optimization should make your system more efficient and enjoyable to use.

Phase Four: Evolution and Mastery

Your final challenge is to demonstrate that your memory system can evolve and adapt over time while maintaining its effectiveness. Implement systematic maintenance protocols that will keep your system sharp and accessible throughout your life. Create regular practice routines, review schedules, and assessment procedures that ensure continuous development.

Develop expansion protocols that allow your system to grow and adapt as your needs change, and your capabilities develop. Plan how you'll add new techniques, expand existing capabilities, and integrate future innovations into your established system.

Create a comprehensive documentation system that captures your memory system's design, protocols, and evolution. This documentation should serve as both a reference for your own use and a foundation for teaching others who might want to learn from your approach.

Demonstrate mastery by applying your complete system to a significant, real-world challenge that requires sustained memory performance over an extended period. This might be a professional project, academic endeavor, or personal learning goal that showcases your system's capabilities and your own transformation into a memory master.

The Master Detective's Revelation: Your Journey to Memory Mastery

Detective 369 stands at his window, looking out at the city lights that sparkle like neural connections in the vast network of human potential. The personal memory system you're about to build, he reflects, represents more than just a collection of techniques–it's a transformation of how you think, learn, and engage with the world around you.

The research is clear and compelling: individuals who develop systematic approaches to memory don't just remember more information–they think more clearly, learn more efficiently, and approach challenges with greater confidence. When you master your own memory, you're not just improving your recall abilities; you're developing the cognitive skills that separate experts from amateurs in any field.

Detective 369 has observed that the most profound changes occur not when you learn individual memory techniques, but when you develop the meta-skills of system design, integration, and optimization. When you can assess your own cognitive capabilities, design personalized approaches to memory challenges, and continuously evolve your methods based on experience, you develop what researchers call "cognitive flexibility"–the ability to adapt your thinking to any situation.

The personal memory system isn't just about professional advantage or academic success–it's about intellectual freedom. Freedom from the anxiety of information overload, freedom from dependence on external memory aids, and freedom to pursue any interest or challenge with confidence in your ability to master the necessary knowledge. These capabilities don't just make you more effective; they make you more intellectually adventurous and personally satisfied.

Perhaps most importantly, the memory system becomes a foundation for lifelong learning and continuous growth. Detective 369 has never stopped developing his memory capabilities, discovering new applications for familiar techniques, and finding novel ways to combine different approaches. Your system should be designed not just for current needs, but for the person you're becoming and the challenges you'll face throughout your life.

The Investigation Concludes: Your Memory Legacy

Detective 369 turns from the window and walks toward the door, his investigation into memory mastery complete but his work far from finished. The techniques he's revealed, the systems he's described, and the transformation he's guided represent the culmination of decades of research, practice, and refinement. They're not just memory tools–they're instruments of cognitive empowerment that can transform how you think, learn, and engage with the world.

The key to long-term success with your personal memory system is understanding that it's not a destination but a journey. Detective 369 has been refining his approach for decades, and he's still discovering new applications and improvements. Your system should be designed for continuous evolution, growing more sophisticated and more perfectly suited to your needs as you develop expertise and encounter new challenges.

Remember that your memory system is ultimately a tool for achieving your goals and living your values. The techniques themselves are means to an end–the end being a more capable, confident, and intellectually empowered version of yourself. Don't get so focused on perfecting techniques that you forget why you're building these capabilities in the first place.

The investment you make in developing your personal memory system will pay dividends throughout your life. The skills you build, the confidence you develop, and the cognitive capabilities you enhance will serve you in every professional and personal challenge you encounter. In an age of information overload and rapid change, the ability to systematically master any knowledge domain isn't just an advantage–it's a necessity.

Detective 369 pauses at the threshold, his hand on the brass doorknob. The fog of cognitive limitation that clouds so many minds begins to clear when you master these memory techniques. Random information becomes organized knowledge, overwhelming complexity becomes manageable challenge, and the vast landscape of human knowledge becomes a territory you can navigate with confidence and precision.

The detective tips his fedora one final time and steps into the morning light. Your Master Detective's Toolkit is now complete, your personal memory system is ready for deployment, and the techniques for lifelong cognitive mastery are in your hands. The investigation into memory techniques has reached its conclusion, but your journey toward intellectual mastery has only just begun.

The cases that once seemed impossibly complex now stand ready to be solved with systematic precision. The information that once threatened to overwhelm now awaits organized integration into your growing knowledge base. The challenges that once seemed beyond your capabilities now become opportunities to demonstrate the power of a truly masterful mind.

Detective 369 has shown you the way, taught you the techniques, and revealed the secrets of memory mastery. Now the investigation continues–not with his guidance, but with your own systematic application of everything you've learned. The toolkit is complete, the system is ready, and the path to memory mastery stretches before you.

The case files are closed, but the investigation never ends. Welcome to the ranks of the memory masters. The city of knowledge awaits your exploration.

The final case file closes with the decisive click of a master detective's toolkit snapping shut. Detective 369 has revealed the ultimate secret: not just how to use memory techniques, but how to build personal systems that transform ordinary minds into extraordinary ones. The investigation is complete, but the journey toward memory mastery begins now, with you as the detective and your own cognitive transformation as the case to be solved.

Case Closed: The Detective's Final Words

The desk lamp casts long shadows across the evidence board as Detective 369 places the final photograph in position. The case that began with a simple question– "How do I remember better?"–has revealed itself to be something far more profound: a complete transformation of how the human mind can operate when given the right tools, the right training, and the right systematic approach.

The investigation is complete, but the case never truly closes.

What began as a simple inquiry into memory improvement has revealed itself to be something far more significant: a blueprint for cognitive transformation that can reshape not just how you remember, but how you think, learn, and engage with the world around you.

You came to this investigation, perhaps, with modest goals. Maybe you wanted to stop forgetting names at networking events. Maybe you needed to master complex professional information. Maybe you simply wanted to feel more confident in your own mental capabilities. But what you've discovered is that memory training isn't just about remembering–it's about becoming.

The techniques you've learned aren't just tools; they're transformative technologies for the mind. The Memory Palace method doesn't just help you store information–it teaches you to think spatially and systematically about knowledge itself. The Major System doesn't just convert numbers to images–it demonstrates the power of systematic encoding to make abstract information concrete and memorable. The linking methods don't just connect facts–they reveal the associative networks that underlie all human understanding.

But perhaps the most important discovery you've made is this: your memory was never broken. It was simply untrained. Every forgotten name, every missed detail, every moment of mental fog–these weren't failures of your cognitive apparatus. They were simply the natural result of trying to use sophisticated mental machinery without understanding how it works.

Now you understand. Now you have the tools. Now you possess the systematic approaches that can transform any information challenge into a manageable, even enjoyable, mental exercise.

The student who once struggled with overwhelming textbooks now builds Memory Palaces where knowledge lives in organized, accessible form. The professional who once fumbled for facts during crucial meetings now commands comprehensive mental databases that respond instantly to any query. The lifelong learner who once felt intimidated by new subjects now approaches unfamiliar domains with confidence, knowing that the right techniques can make any information memorable.

This transformation didn't happen by accident. It happened because you learned to think like a detective about your own memory. You learned to treat information like evidence, to approach forgetting like a mystery to be solved, and to view your mind as a precision instrument that responds to systematic training.

The techniques you've mastered will serve you for a lifetime, but they're not static tools. They're living systems that will grow and adapt with you as your needs change, and your expertise develops. The Memory Palace you build today will expand tomorrow. The peg systems you've learned will accommodate new types of information as you encounter them. The associative networks you've developed will continue to strengthen and elaborate as you apply them to new domains.

But remember this: mastery isn't a destination–it's a direction. The memory masters who inspire awe aren't those who learned techniques once and considered themselves finished. They're those who continue to practice, to refine, to discover new applications for familiar methods. They understand that cognitive excellence, like physical fitness, requires ongoing attention and systematic maintenance.

The fog that once obscured your mental capabilities has lifted. The scattered evidence of your intellectual life has been organized into systematic knowledge. The mystery of how to remember has been solved, but the investigation into what you can accomplish with a trained memory has only just begun.

Your case files are organized. Your techniques are proven. Your mental toolkit is complete.

The city of knowledge spreads before you, no longer shrouded in the fog of forgetfulness, but illuminated by the clear light of systematic memory mastery. Every street is navigable, every building is accessible, every piece of information is within reach of your trained mind.

The investigation continues. The mysteries multiply. The tools are in your hands.

Detective 369 tips his fedora, adjusts his coat against the night air, and steps into the foggy streets. Another case closed. Another mind transformed. Another victory for the power of systematic memory training.

The city sleeps, but the memory never rests.

Case Closed.

> "The best detectives aren't those who solve the most cases–they're those who teach others to solve their own mysteries."
>
> –Detective 369

References

Baddeley, A. D. (2000). The episodic buffer: A new component of working memory? Trends in Cognitive Sciences, 4(11), 417–423.

Bower, G. H. (1970). Analysis of a mnemonic device. American Scientist, 58(5), 496–510.

Burgess, N., Maguire, E. A., & O'Keefe, J. (2002). The human hippocampus and spatial and episodic memory. Neuron, 35(4), 625–641.

Cepeda, N. J., Pashler, H., Vul, E., Wixted, J. T., & Rohrer, D. (2006). Distributed practice in verbal recall tasks: A review and quantitative synthesis. Psychological Bulletin, 132(3), 354–380.

Craik, F. I. M., & Lockhart, R. S. (1972). Levels of processing: A framework for memory research. Journal of Verbal Learning and Verbal Behavior, 11(6), 671–684.

Higbee, K. L. (1977). Your memory: How it works and how to improve it. Prentice Hall.

Karpicke, J. D., & Blunt, J. R. (2011). Retrieval practice produces more learning than elaborative studying with concept mapping. Science, 331(6018), 772–775.

Lorayne, H., & Lucas, J. (1974). The memory book: The classic guide to improving your memory at work, at school, and at play. Ballantine Books.

Maguire, E. A., Gadian, D. G., Johnsrude, I. S., Good, C. D., Ashburner, J., Frackowiak, R. S., & Frith, C. D. (2000). Navigation-related structural change in the hippocampi of taxi drivers. Proceedings of the National Academy of Sciences, 97(8), 4398–4403.

Miller, G. A. (1956). The magical number seven, plus or minus two: Some limits on our capacity for processing information. Psychological Review, 63(2), 81–97.

O'Keefe, J., & Nadel, L. (1978). The hippocampus as a cognitive map. Oxford University Press.

Paivio, A. (1971). Imagery and verbal processes. Holt, Rinehart & Winston.

Roediger, H. L., & Butler, A. C. (2011). The critical role of retrieval practice in long-term retention. Trends in Cognitive Sciences, 15(1), 20–27.

Roediger, H. L., & Karpicke, J. D. (2006). Test-enhanced learning: Taking memory tests improves long-term retention. Psychological Science, 17(3), 249–255.

Standing, L. (1973). Learning 10,000 pictures. Quarterly Journal of Experimental Psychology, 25(2), 207–222.

Tulving, E. (1985). Memory and consciousness. Canadian Psychology, 26(1), 1–12.

Wozniak, P. A., & Gorzelanczyk, E. J. (1994). Optimization of learning by practice. International Journal of Educational Research, 21(8), 869–882.

Appendix A: Alphabet PEG Systems

Instructions

1. **Learn the Peg Images:** Familiarize yourself with the image or word associated with each letter of the alphabet (see the table below).
2. **Practice Visualization:** When you need to recall or imagine a letter, think of its corresponding image. For example, if you think of the letter "C," picture a cat.
3. **Associate Items as Needed:** If you have a list to remember, link each item to the image for its corresponding letter. For instance, if the third item is "apple," associate it with "Cat" (the peg for C), perhaps by imagining an apple with cat ears and a tail.
4. **Recall by Letter:** To recall your list, go through the alphabet and visualize each peg image. The image will trigger the associated item.
5. **Use for Any Purpose:** You can use this system to remember anything that can be ordered by letter—shopping lists, steps in a process, names, or even as a way to practice letter recognition and association.

Note: The Alphabet PEG list (A–Z) uses intuitive image associations for each letter (e.g., A = Apple, B = Ball). It is *not* based on the Major System and is intended as a beginner-friendly mnemonic tool.

Alphabet Table

Letter	Sequence Number	Sample Peg Image (Commonly Used)
A	1	Apple
B	2	Balloon
C	3	Cat
D	4	Dog
E	5	Elephant
F	6	Fish
G	7	Guitar
H	8	House
I	9	Ice

Letter	Sequence Number	Sample Peg Image (Commonly Used)
J	10	Jar
K	11	Kite
L	12	Lamp
M	13	Moon
N	14	Nest
O	15	Orange
P	16	Pencil
Q	17	Queen
R	18	Rose
S	19	Ship
T	20	Tree
U	21	Umbrella
V	22	Violin
W	23	Watch
X	24	Xylophone
Y	25	Yacht
Z	26	Zebra

Appendix B: Major System Table

The Major System is a mnemonic technique that transforms numbers into memorable words by converting each digit into specific consonant sounds. This system, widely used by memory champions and popularized by Harry Lorayne & Jerry Lucas, allows you to encode and recall long sequences of numbers with ease.

Number-to-Sound Table

Digit	Consonant Sounds (Phonetics)	Example Letters
0	/s/, /z/	s, z, soft c
1	/t/, /d/, /θ/, /ð/	t, d, th (thing, this)
2	/n/	n
3	/m/	m
4	/r/	r
5	/l/	l
6	/tʃ/, /dʒ/, /ʃ/, /ʒ/	ch, j, sh, soft g
7	/k/, /g/	k, hard c, g, q, ck
8	/f/, /v/	f, v, ph
9	/p/, /b/	p, b

Rules for Translating Numbers to Words

1. **Do Not Translate Vowels:** Vowels (a, e, i, o, u) are not assigned to any number and are ignored. They act as "fillers" to help form meaningful words.
2. **Ignore Semivowels and Certain Consonants:** The letters **h, w, y** are not assigned to any number and are ignored.
3. **Focus on Sounds, Not Spelling:** The mapping is based on how words sound, not how they are spelled. For example, "action" is 762 (/k/-/ʃ/-/n/), not 712.
4. **Double Letters Count as One Sound:** Double letters are only counted once unless they are pronounced separately (e.g., "butter" is 914, but "midday" is 311).

5. **Silent Letters Are Ignored:** Any letter that is silent does not count in the translation (e.g., the "k" in "knee" is silent, so the word is just 2).
6. **Special Cases for Certain Letters:**
   - **"x"** is usually treated as two sounds, K-S, making it 70.
   - **"q"** is usually treated as K, making it **7.**
   - **"gh"** is usually ignored unless pronounced as F (e.g., "enough" is 28).

Example Translation

Let's translate the number **0151:** * **0** → s * **1** → t * **5** → l * **1** → t

By adding vowels, a possible word is **satellite** (s-t-l-t).

Additional Tips

- **Consistency is Key:** Use your chosen mappings and rules consistently for the best results.
- **Make It Personal:** Choose words and images that are meaningful or memorable to you.
- **Practice:** Regular practice will make translation faster and more automatic.

By following these rules and using the provided table, you can turn any number into a memorable word or phrase, making it much easier to remember long sequences of digits.

Sources & Further Reading

- Mnemonic major system - Wikipedia https://en.wikipedia.org/wiki/Mnemonic_major_system
- Lorayne, H., & Lucas, J. (1974). *The memory book: The classic guide to improving your memory at work, at school, and at play.* Ballantine Books.
- Art of Memory - How to Memorize Numbers with the Major System https://artofmemory.com/blog/major-system/

Appendix C: Sample 0-9 PEGS

Number	Major Sound	PEG Word	Explanation
0	S / Z	Sew	S = 0
1	T / D	Tie	T = 1
2	N	Noah	N = 2
3	M	Ma	M = 3
4	R	Ray	R = 4
5	L	Law	L = 5
6	J / SH / CH	Shoe	SH = 6
7	K / G (hard)	Cow	K = 7
8	F / V	Ivy	V = 8
9	P / B	Bee	B = 9

Appendix D: The 100-PEG System (00-99)

Below is a list of mnemonic pegs built using the Major System. Each number from 00 to 99 is assigned a memorable word. Use this reference to construct peg lists or mental filing systems.

Number	Mnemonic Word	Number	Mnemonic Word
00	Sauce	50	Lace
01	Suit	51	Lid
02	Sun	52	Lion
03	Sum	53	Lamb
04	Sore	54	Lure
05	Seal	55	Lily
06	Sash	56	Leech
07	Socks	57	Log
08	Sofa	58	Leaf
09	Soap	59	Lip
10	Toes	60	Chess
11	Toad	61	Jet
12	Tin	62	Chain
13	Dime	63	Jam
14	Tire	64	Cherry
15	Tile	65	Jewel
16	Dish	66	Judge
17	Duck	67	Chalk
18	Dove	68	Chef
19	Tape	69	Ship
20	Nose	70	Case
21	Net	71	Cat
22	Nun	72	Can
23	Name	73	Comb
24	Nero	74	Car
25	Nail	75	Coal

Number	Mnemonic Word	Number	Mnemonic Word
26	Notch	76	Cage
27	Neck	77	Cake
28	Knife	78	Cave
29	Nub	79	Cap
30	Moss	80	Vase
31	Mat	81	Foot
32	Moon	82	Fan
33	Mummy	83	Foam
34	Mower	84	Fur
35	Mule	85	File
36	Match	86	Fish
37	Mug	87	Fig
38	Movie	88	Fife
39	Map	89	Fib
40	Rose	90	Bus
41	Road	91	Bat
42	Rain	92	Bone
43	Room	93	Beam
44	Rower	94	Bear
45	Rail	95	Bell
46	Rash	96	Bush
47	Rock	97	Book
48	Roof	98	Beef
49	Rope	99	Pipe

Publication & Legal Notices

Reader Responsibility Statement

Disclaimer

The information contained in this book is for informational and educational purposes only. The content is not intended to be a substitute for professional advice, diagnosis, or treatment in any field. The memory techniques, methods, and strategies presented in this book are based on established principles and the author's research and experience.

Educational Purpose Only

This book is designed to provide general information about memory improvement techniques and learning strategies. The author and publisher make no representations or warranties of any kind with respect to the accuracy, applicability, fitness, or completeness of the contents of this book.

No Liability

Published by Existential Publishing, edited by Timothy McManus. We assume no liability or responsibility for any errors, omissions, or consequences arising from the use of the information contained herein. Under no circumstances shall the author or publisher be liable for any direct, indirect, incidental, special, or consequential damages resulting from the use of this book or the techniques described within.

Individual Results May Vary

The effectiveness of memory techniques varies from person to person. While the methods presented in this book are based on established principles and research, individual results cannot be guaranteed. Readers are encouraged to practice these techniques responsibly and adapt them to their individual needs and circumstances.

Use at Your Own Risk

By reading and using this book, you acknowledge that you do so at your own risk and that you are solely responsible for any consequences that may arise from implementing the techniques described herein. If you have specific concerns about your memory, learning abilities, or cognitive function, please consult with qualified professionals in the appropriate fields.

Credits

Cover art and interior design by Existential Publishing. AI tools were used in the creation of some illustrations under direct human supervision. All images are original or used with proper license. AI tools were used to assist in research and creating text, under human supervision with extensive human editing.

Revisions

Date	Notes	By
2025-08-16	Corrected heading hierarchy; tightened TOC (H1–H2 only).	Todd Hearst
2025-08-12	Migrated to Markdown; added build script; first full editorial pass.	Todd Hearst
2025-07-31	Fixed formatting issues and pagination for chapter openers.	Todd Hearst

Connect with the Author

- **Email:** manager@existential-publishing.com
- **Newsletter & Blog:** www.existential-publishing.com
- **YouTube:** youtube.com/@ExistentialDetective369
- **BlueSky:** @existential-publishing.bsky.social

Stay informed about new books, tutorials, and memory training tools.